John Kersley Fowler

Recollections of Old Country Life

Social, Political, Sporting and Agricultural

John Kersley Fowler

Recollections of Old Country Life

Social, Political, Sporting and Agricultural

ISBN/EAN: 9783337078737

Printed in Europe, USA, Canada, Australia, Japan

Cover: Foto ©Suzi / pixelio.de

More available books at **www.hansebooks.com**

RECOLLECTIONS

OF

OLD COUNTRY LIFE

SOCIAL, POLITICAL, SPORTING, & AGRICULTURAL

By J. K. FOWLER ('RUSTICUS')
formerly of Aylesbury
AUTHOR OF 'ECHOES OF OLD COUNTY LIFE'

'All men are interested in any man if he will speak the facts of his life for them; his authentic experience, which corresponds as face to face to that of all other sons of Adam'—LORD RONALD GOWER

LONDON
LONGMANS, GREEN, AND CO.
AND NEW YORK: 15 EAST 16th STREET
1894

All rights reserved

TO MARY

MY DEARLY LOVED WIFE

THE MOTHER OF MY TEN LIVING CHILDREN

AND FOR NEARLY FIFTY YEARS

THE PARTNER OF MY SORROWS AND MY JOY

I DEDICATE THIS BOOK

CONTENTS

CHAPTER I

PAGE

Introductory—Squire Drake—Master of Bicester Hunt—His opinion of the House of Commons—H.R.H. the Prince of Wales—Sir Anthony Rothschild—Bucks election—The squire's liberality to his tenants—Tom Wingfield—Borough of Amersham—Lady Verney—The great election for Bucks in 1784—How election success is lost—Ashridge tenants—Final state of the poll . . 1

CHAPTER II

Camden Neild—His gift to the Queen—A Welsh coal-owner and iron-master—Bernal Osborne—Mentmore—'Conticuere omnes'—Kerry cattle—An Irish tale of a fox—Mrs. S. C. Hall's story—Lord Charles Russell, Mr. Perkins, and M.C.C. and W. G. Grace 10

CHAPTER III

John Hampden—His death—Chalgrove Field—Exhumation of his body—Sacrilegious conduct of Lord Nugent and others—Desecration of the remains of the great patriot—Identification of his body—His portrait—Robertson, of Hampden Gardens—Jasper More—Visit to Roman Gravels mine—Address to the miners—Prizes for hillside allotments—Lord Clive—Emperor Hadrian's mine 17

CHAPTER IV

Volunteers—Amersham Yeoman—Anecdote of a solicitor—Sporting customs of gormandising—Amersham v. Beaconsfield—Parish rivalries—Boiled beef and concomitants—Vinegar—Triumphant return home—Prize-fight between Tom Hatton and Mickey Gannon—The Archdeacon's opinions—Jem Mace, Champion of England—London and North-Western Railway—

Anecdote of tenant of Denbigh Hall—Prevention of an accident—A visit to Hughenden—A wreath on the great statesman's grave—The visit of the Queen—The casket placed on his tomb—and final closing of tomb—Anecdote of Devonshire rector—The 'Saddling Bell'—A Northumberland rector's ride to church—Sports of the field at Oxford—An Oxford undergraduate is plucked on his divinity—The 'Pluck' coach 28

CHAPTER V

Restoration of chancel in Aylesbury Church—A rector's economical suggestion of a slated roof—Prebend of Lincoln—Steeple-chasing—The old Broughton country—Jem Mason and William Archer—'Varsity riders in the 'Fifties'—A dead heat and heavy stakes with Tom Price and Ned Enoch—Charlie and George Symonds—Joe Tollit—Perrin's old horse Phœnix—The Pratt Club—and Grand National Hunt Steeplechases—Over Prebendal Farm—Lowlander's first appearance—and after performances 37

CHAPTER VI

Harry Poole—Count d'Orsay—Napoleon III.—Mr. Pennington, High Sheriff of Bucks—and the grand fête at Cherbourg—Lord Beaconsfield — 'Lothair' — The FitzClarences — The King's, Mr. De Burgh's, and Rothschild's staghounds—Cliveden—Duchess of Sutherland—Brahmin cow—Cattle show—Spring gardening—The Duchess and Fleming—Sewage irrigation—Maplin Sands—Prince Albert's plan—Mr. Yarrow—Peat charcoal.—Osiers 44

CHAPTER VII

The Lowndes family—and Whaddon lawsuit—'The Writ of Right'—The reading of a tombstone—Serjeant Talfourd, afterwards a judge—Two dormant peerages—Whaddon Chase—Finding of Cymbeline British gold coins—The Kimbles—Great Roman Road—The Icknield Way, or Via Iceni—Bishop Wilberforce—An American's visit to the Chilterns—Visit to Ireland—An Irish agriculturist on the growth of beans—Rathkeale—'Greville Memoirs'—Account of Ireland 56

CHAPTER VIII

Judges and the Bar—Lawsuit—London and North-Western Railway —Horace Lloyd—Staveley Hill—'The Straits of Malacca'—Lord Chief Justice Cockburn—and Mr. Serjeant Wells—Cock-fighting —The billeting of soldiers in an assize town—Lord Chief Baron Pollock—The advent of judges to the assize towns past and present—Pedigree of Duke of Buckingham and Chandos—Charles Brandon, Duke of Suffolk—Marriage of Mary Tudor with Louis XII.—Public entry into Paris—Great rejoicing—Jousts and Tournaments—Charles Brandon and English knights distinguish themselves—The Duke d'Alençon—Numbers of knights at the tournament—Charles Brandon unhorses the German giant— Death of the king—Marriage of Duke of Suffolk with the widowed queen—Return to England—Anecdote of great descent   64

CHAPTER IX

Volunteers—My connection with the movement—Long service decoration as Quartermaster—Encampments—The Eton volunteers —Major Warre—Quartermaster Hale—The water drill—Gallant advance by swimming the Thames—Water polo—Capt. Durnford —Edwards-Moss—Remarkable trials—The Burnham murder— Moses Hatto—His death sentence—Curious circumstantial evidence—Jemmy Brookes, imprisonment for life—Duke of Buckingham's sword—Stealing a shroud—Sacrilegious robbery of lead from coffins—Jones, the Denham murderer—Coaching and Needle's murder—Horse-stealing—Soda and brandy .   .   .   74

CHAPTER X

Gastronomy—Mr. John Kaye—High Sheriff—His dinner—The Trafalgar at Greenwich—Emperor sherry—Whitebait—Mr. Hart —Baron Meyer de Rothschild—James McConnell—Floral decorations—Railway banquet—Mr. H. W. Lawson's coming of age—Late Henry Brassey—Lord Mayor's banquet at the Mansion House—Luncheon at the Kalenberg, Vienna—and bills of fare   92

xii RECOLLECTIONS OF OLD COUNTRY LIFE

CHAPTER XI

PAGE

Journey to Bordeaux—Orleans—Château de Blois, Chambord, Chenonceaux, d'Amboise, &c.—St. Cross and the Dole—Marshal Saxe—' Les Landes '—Biarritz—Sea-bathing—Fontarabia—Pau—Bordeaux—Foreign opinion of cattle, &c.—Letters from Moët and Johnston 109

CHAPTER XII

George Stephenson and Delmé Radcliffe on railways—Vienna Exhibition—My cattle—Nuremberg—Albert Dürer—Sir A. de Rothschild—Voyage down the Danube—Blondel and Richard Cœur de Lion—A sword-swallower—The Emperor Franz Joseph—The Crown Prince Rudolph—Baron Albert de Rothschild—Procrastination—The Tyrol—Salzburg—Judging at Agricultural Shows—Manchester—Drying hay—Churns and dairy appliances—Kilburn—Foreign cattle—Ensilage—Altona—Schleswig-Holstein—H. Corbet 124

CHAPTER XIII

Steam cultivation—Advance in agricultural pursuits—Costume—Story of a smock frock—Poultry-farming—Cochins, &c.—Statistics of poultry-keeping—The rinderpest—Old Fuchsia and her progeny—Immense prices—The bull Earl of Darlington built up in a faggot pile—John Clayden of Littlebury—and Home Cattle Defence Association—Quotation of Virgil and rinderpest—Marshal MacMahon—M. Tisserand de Bort at Paris Exhibition—Fashion at the dinner-table 141

CHAPTER XIV

Mr. Robert Ceely—Vaccination experiments—The night-flowering cereus—The agricultural labourer—His varied occupations—His wages—Pleasures of agricultural life—The effect of railways on agriculture 157

CHAPTER XV

The Rothschild family—They settle in Bucks—Establishment of the staghounds—Opposition of Duke of Buckingham—Judæa—A romantic 'Varsity story—Inter-'Varsity steeplechases—Point-to-point 'chases—Ladies hunting—Empress of Austria . . . 166

CHAPTER XVI

The agricultural labourer—Advantages of a wooden leg—Sermon on optics—Short-horn breeding—Bates and Booth breeds—Mr. Adkins of Milcote—High prices for short-horns 184

CHAPTER XVII

Tombstones and their inscriptions—Some ancient—Illiterate spelling—A citizen of Taunton—The Lee Monument 1584—Clever and learned at Munich—Severe inscription at Luton—John Wilkes's gardener—Lady O'Looney—Lockyer and his pills, with others in St. Saviour's, Southwark—Quarrendon Chapel and its wanton destruction 192

CHAPTER XVIII

A terrible parricide—Singular evidence—Fitzroy Kelly and the missing pocket-book—'Adding Fuel to fire'—The verdict—Chequers Court and the Kimbles—Similarity of pedigree of Charles I. and Cromwell—Anne Hyde, mother of two queens—Reminiscences of jockeys—Old Bob Barker 210

CHAPTER XIX

Agricultural visits to the Continent—Manufacture of sugar from beetroot—Farming at Genappe and Waterloo—Ireland as a field for sugar—Dr. Shack Sommer—Statistics of saccharine—percentage in roots—Clarendon, Greville, and Thackeray on the Irish peasantry—Dean Hole on roses—Sappho and the rose—Royal Agricultural Show at Windsor—Jubilee life members—Sixty Years' retrospect 222

LIST OF ILLUSTRATIONS

JOHN KERSLEY FOWLER, V.D., QUARTERMASTER, BUCKS
   VOLUNTEERS . . . . *Frontispiece*
SQUIRE DRAKE OF SHARDELOES AND HIS HUNTSMAN
   TOM WINGFIELD, AND BEN GODDARD, FIRST WHIP . *page* xxii
HAMPDEN HOUSE, THE SEAT OF THE EARL OF BUCKING-
   HAMSHIRE . . . . ,, 17
OLD ENTRANCE LODGES AND QUEEN'S GAP AT HAMPDEN ,, 24
THE DEAD HEAT . . . . ,, 40
GROUP OF OFFICERS OF BUCKS VOLUNTEERS . . . ,, 75
THE WHITE HART, GARDEN FRONT, SHOWING THE
   PORTION BUILT BY THE EARL OF ROCHESTER IN 1663 ,, 107
WHITE HART AND COUNTY HALL, STREET FRONT . . ,, 140
THE BARON'S HOUNDS AT MENTMORE . . . . ,, 168
FRED COX AND LORD ROTHSCHILD'S HOUNDS AT TRING
   PARK . . . . ,, 173
THE OLD MARKET-PLACE, AYLESBURY . . . ,, 219

NOTE.

With the exception of the Frontispiece and the Plate of 'Dead Heat,' all the Illustrations are reproduced from Photographs kindly lent by Mr. S. G. Payne, of Aylesbury.

INTRODUCTION

It is generally expected by the public that, in publishing the memoirs or recollections of one's own life, some account should be given of the family history of the author, and as my excuse for so doing I quote what Walter Besant remarks on the subject. In one of his novels, 'They were Married,' he says:

> It is a fine thing for a great house whose history has been preserved. It makes one weep to think how our middle-class people neglect their genealogies, so that they know nothing of their own people, and have no pride, and learn no lesson from the past. Cannot something be done, my friends? Can we not write the annals of our own generation? Each of his own family, so that whatever the fate of our children and grandchildren, they, too, may feel that they have ancestors who lived, and loved, and hoped, and made a little success, perhaps, and died, and were forgotten, as they, too, in their turns shall die? Generally the women of the house keep up its memories, not the men. That matters nothing, if they were true to their name and its ambitions.

It has been somewhere said that men when speaking of their family tree are fond of descanting on the noble timbers cut from the oak, but seldom care to record the chips that fly from those timbers, or the stray knots and decayed branches which also belonged to the tree. However, I may say that the line of 'Fowlers' from whom I am descended are a very ancient family, and trace back to the time of Richard Cœur de Lion. Some years since a Mr. Fowler Carter, a student at Lincoln College, Oxford, applied to me to give him some idea of the source from which our family sprang. I found him a most intelligent and learned genealogical student, and he then stated, I believe correctly, that our branch was descended from a Sir Richard Fowler, whose recumbent figure lies on a tomb in Tilsworth Church, Bedfordshire, which is about fourteen miles from Aylesbury. My father knew that one of the Tilsworth Fowlers settled near to Chipping Norton, and founded the Gloucestershire family; and that a cadet of the Chipping Norton branch settled in Hampshire, about the middle of the seventeenth century, at the village of Hinton, near Bramdean in that county; and I have seen the tombstones of these Fowlers, from 1680 onwards, and the last of the line lived at the 'Woodlands' in that parish. He died somewhere about the year 1820; his name was Charles, and he was the last of a family of eight sons and two daughters. One of the latter I remember perfectly well—an old lady, a widow—named Brittain. I knew her as cousin 'Nanny'; she died about 1828, outliving old Charlie. There was a sum of about 5,000*l*., the remains of the family estate, which was left to my father and two uncles. There were twelve apostle spoons, the remnant of the family plate, which had belonged to a sister of Bishop White, the last Romish bishop of Winchester, and it was said were given to her by her brother, and from this lady we were descended. These spoons were quite unique, they bore the Hall mark of 1529, and I believe are the only known specimens of that date. Unfortunately Charles Fowler divided them, and left them between other members of the family, but eight of them were obtained, and were sold at Christie's about eighteen months since at the enormous sum of 260 guineas, or about 32*l. per ounce* ! The father of this large family was William Fowler, a staunch old Royalist, who made his family fall on their knees before retiring to rest and pray for Prince Charlie ; he scorned the idea of his being called ' The Pretender,' and said the Hanoverian princes were the '*Pretenders*.' My great-grandfather was the son of one of these old Tories, and came into Buckinghamshire, settled at Amersham, and became a tenant of the Drakes, holding the principal inn in that ancient borough, with a large farm nearly adjoining which was attached to it. For about a century the Fowlers held this property. My father when twenty-one years of age left the paternal roof, and came to Aylesbury in 1812, and four years afterwards married a Miss Complin, my mother, a remarkably beautiful woman, the daughter of a substantial yeoman living at Preston Candover, near Alresford. They were second cousins, through the family of the Kersleys, who were considered as 'founder's kin' of William of Wykeham, and they had a right of presentation to Winchester College School, also to New College, Oxford, and bore the family motto of 'Manners makyth man.' I remember after my uncle Charles (my father's brother) gave up the tenancy of Amersham, and went to Banbury, the well-known provost of Eton, Dr. Goodall, came to my father's house at Aylesbury one day—as he was on the road to his brother's, the Rev. Joseph Goodall, of Dinton, about five miles further—and the learned provost said to me, 'So your family at last have left Amersham.' I replied, 'Yes, sir ; they have been tenants of the Drakes for a hundred years.'

'Gently, young gentleman,' he said, 'do not give way to exaggeration, for I have found it all out; it is not a hundred years, it is only *ninety-eight*,' and he leaned back in his carriage and laughed heartily.

But I must now return to the old family history from Sir Richard of Tilsworth. It is somewhat remarkable that a few months since (June 1893) I received a letter from a Mr. William Fowler, of Milford, Connecticut, U.S.A., in which he says, 'I have seen in the "New York Tribune" a very flattering review of a book called "Echoes of old County Life" written by you, and Messrs. Macmillan have furnished me with your address,' and he wished to know about my ancestry, and sent me what was known of his which he had published in a pamphlet which he had sent me, beautifully printed, called an 'Historical Sketch and Genealogical Record of the Fowlers of Milford, Connecticut, U.S.A.,' by John William Fowler, and its first page is headed 'Some Account of the Fowlers of Buckinghamshire in England.' After describing how the name of Fowler arose, for it designated the calling as 'Fowler to the King,' or 'Fowler to de Guader, Earl of Norfolk,' and that it was the same as Anglo-Saxon Fugelere, German *Vogeler*, a birdcatcher, he goes on to say that the name of Rychard Fowller is mentioned in the chronicles of the English Crusaders among the Anglo-Norman knights, who took part in the expedition under Richard Cœur de Lion. Burke affirms the great antiquity of the Fowler family before the time of Richard I. The chronicle commences from Sir Richard le Fowlere, 1190, who held large estates in Bucks, and that he accompanied Richard to the Holy Land, and that during the crusade he maintained a body of British bowmen, all his own tenants, and at the siege of Acre he defeated by his extraordinary vigilance a nocturnal attempt of Saladin to surprise the British camp; and for these services he was knighted by Richard on the field of battle, and ordered thereafter to wear a new crest, viz. 'the vigilant Owl' (see Kimber, iii. 1113). This Sir Richard Fowler, the Crusader, was progenitor of a family the main stock of which flourished in Bucks for over five hundred years. Henry Fowler de Foxley, Esq., was in the retinue of Henry V. at Agincourt, 1415, to which battle he brought two foot-archers; this Henry was member of Parliament for Bucks, and afterwards for Chipping Wycombe. In the reign of Edward IV. Sir Richard was Chancellor of the Duchy of Lancaster, and represented Bucks in Parliament. This gentleman and his descendants held several manors in Bucks, and in the time of Elizabeth one of the family lived on his property at Aylesbury. From the Aylesbury Fowlers sprang the American branch at Milford. These left England in the 'Mayflower,' and settled about 1637 at Milford, where they have resided ever since. Edward Fowler, son of the Chancellor, entertained Queen Katherine at Boreton, near Buckingham, and was gentleman of the bedchamber to Edward VI. He inherited large estates in Bucks, and died in 1541. His second son Roger, styled De Broomhill, county Norfolk, fought in the Scottish wars in 1514. He married Cecilia Lee, of the family of Sir Andrew Trollop, a doughty soldier who fought in the Lancastrian wars, and fell at Towton. She (Cecilia Lee) was sister to the Rev. Rowland Lee, the chaplain to Henry VIII. who performed the marriage ceremony between that monarch and Anne Boleyn. He was afterwards consecrated Bishop of Lichfield and Coventry, and at his death bequeathed his property to his nephews, sons of Roger Fowler.

From the above family records it would appear that Mr. Fowler Carter's surmises were perfectly correct, and they were established through the remarkable circumstance of Mr. William Fowler reading my book in America. This is another illustration that our brethren across the water are proud of their descent from old English families; and I have often been told that, if it were not for our American cousins continually searching for arms, our Heralds' College might soon close its doors. From studying this remarkable pedigree it shows what has often been stated by several eminent writers, that the fame of a distinguished family may lie dormant for many years, even a century, but by some fortuitous circumstances it may be revived again, with even more distinction than it had hitherto enjoyed. My esteemed friend, Sir John Fowler, is descended probably from one of these old fellows; and his marvellous engineering works, the 'Underground Railway' and 'the stupendous Forth Bridge,' are examples that may rival in fame and be of more importance than the salvation of the army of that doughty monarch, Richard Cœur de Lion. And the baronetcy which he received was probably as well deserved as the knighthood Sir Richard Fowler received on the Field of Ascalon.

SQUIRE DRAKE OF SHARDELOES AND HIS HUNTSMAN TOM WINGFIELD, AND BEN GODDARD, FIRST WHIP
(Painted by William and Henry Barraud, 1846)

FURTHER RECOLLECTIONS

OF

OLD COUNTRY LIFE

CHAPTER I

Introductory—Squire Drake—Master of Bicester Hunt—His opinion of the House of Commons—H.R.H. the Prince of Wales—Sir Anthony Rothschild—Bucks election—The squire's liberality to his tenants—Tom Wingfield—Borough of Amersham—Lady Verney—The great election for Bucks in 1784—How election success is lost—Ashridge tenants—Final state of the poll.

AMONGST the distinguished families in Bucks whom I had the privilege of knowing, none stands more preeminent than the Drakes of Shardeloes, near Amersham. The family settled in this ancient borough in or about the year 1620, and until the disfranchisement of the ancient borough of 'Agmondesham' in 1832, I believe one of the family was enrolled in every Parliament. I remember the old squire, Thomas Tyrwhitt Drake, in my earliest childhood, and afterwards as successor to Sir Thomas Mostyn in the mastership of the Bicester and Wanden

Hill foxhounds. He was a stern, determined man, and a scrupulously good landlord, and had a family of ten children.

His eldest son, Thomas Tyrwhitt, was the genial country squire, and was twice master of the Bicester Hunt, and one of the best men across country it has ever been my lot to follow, or I ought to say *attempt to follow*, for he must have been a hard goer and a bruising rider who could follow the squire for thirty minutes after a fox from Ham Green covert, especially if he pointed over the Vale of Aylesbury.

Many a good story have I heard of Squire Drake, and one in particular was so characteristic that I should like to record it. At the death of the first Lord Chesham a vacancy was created for the representation of the county in Parliament, and a general desire was expressed by all classes that Mr. Drake should be asked to stand for the vacant seat. We all knew his reluctance to enter Parliament, and Mr. Baynes, clerk of the peace for the county, a rare veteran light-weight across country, and myself rode over to the meet at Ham Green to solicit him to allow himself to be nominated. He strongly refused. We put it to him that it should not cost him a penny, that law costs should be provided, and that every farmer in the county would find wagons and horses to bring men to the poll, and that success was certain. After listening to all we had to say, he replied, 'You two fellows have known me all your lives, haven't you?' 'Yes,' we answered. 'Well, you know I have always associated with gentlemen?' 'Certainly.' 'Then why the deuce do you want to send me to the

House of Commons?' He then spurred his horse, galloped down one of the rides of Tittershall Wood, and viewed the fox away, and that was the last attempt made to nominate him for Parliament.

When the Prince of Wales was at Oxford he was always fond of going to the meets of the Bicester Hunt, and of talking with the cheery squire. On one occasion the Prince's nags were not fit to hunt, and he went to old Charley Symond's stables for a horse. All his best 'gees' were engaged; but there was in the stable a rare old screw, a fine goer across country, and his Royal Highness engaged him. I believe the meet was at Arncot Wood. A fox was soon found, and the hounds went away at a merry pace, the squire, as usual, cutting out the running. The Prince, who then went uncommonly well, followed in his wake. The fox took over a very severe country, and, when a check took place, the Prince was one of the first up. The squire rode up to him, and praised him for his pluck. 'I know,' he said, 'the horse you're on; he is a real good 'un, but a screw, and he is very likely to bring you to grief. I have seen you bravely following me; but—I know you'll excuse me—I must as master ride up to my hounds. I may lead you into trouble; I would advise you not to follow me.' The Prince smiled. The hounds again picked up the scent, and after a racing twenty minutes pulled him down in the open at the foot of Brill Hill. The squire looked round, and amongst the very first up was the Prince, all safe and well. He gave him the brush as a reward of merit for his plucky riding. Amongst the distinguished guests of the Prince who dine with him on the Derby Day, Tom Drake was always one.

Sometimes, when the Baron's hounds met near the Bicester country—which ran up to within a mile of Aylesbury—I have known the two packs clash, and dire would be the language of the rival huntsmen, as also of the followers of the two packs, as there was always a great difficulty in separating the hounds. I was out once when this occurred, and old Sir Anthony Rothschild was in charge of the 'staggers.' The scent was bad, and the hunting slow. Mr. Drake was much troubled, but always in a good humour. Sir Anthony said, 'No schent to-day, squire.' The squire replied: 'No, Sir Anthony, the shent is not half so strong as the three-per-shents in the City.'

Lord Beaconsfield, soon after his elevation to the peerage, wrote to me for my opinion as to the result of the forthcoming election for his vacant seat. I told him, in a long letter, that his presence at our agricultural meeting, which was to take place the day before the poll, would make 300 votes difference to us; and he told me afterwards that Tom Drake had ridden over to Hughenden and persuaded him to come, telling him exactly what I had said. The Hon. T. Fremantle, now Lord Cottesloe, was the Tory candidate, and the Hon. Rupert Carrington was the Liberal, and the former was elected by a majority of 187. Lord Carrington had been sanguine of winning the seat for his brother, and he and all his party were very confident. I was told by a friend of mine at Wycombe that a week or two after the election his lordship had remarked to him that they felt sure of winning, 'but the old man's speech at

Aylesbury the day before the poll beat them;' and in conversation with Mr. Drake some time afterwards we agreed that this was so, and we congratulated ourselves on the part we had taken in the result.

I don't think a kinder-hearted man than the squire of Shardeloes ever existed. When the cattle plague, 'the rinderpest,' broke out in Cheshire, the tenants on his extensive estates there suffered terrible loss. The squire directed his agent to give all his tenants a receipt in full for their rents, and took nothing, thus saving them many thousands of pounds wherewith to cover their losses. On another occasion one of his principal tenants at Amersham had failed, owing him nearly 700*l*. rent. The squire gave it all up to the other creditors, as he did not wish that they should lose anything by a tenant of his.

My family had been tenants of the Drakes for over a hundred years, and I have heard my father and grandfather say there never was a bad man in the whole family. The squire was a good agriculturist, and at one time had a fine herd of pedigree shorthorns and a flock of first-class Southdown sheep. His principal tenant on the Lincolnshire property was the well-known 'Billy Torr' of Aylesby Manor, one of the most active members of the Royal Agricultural Society. The latter had a fine herd of Booth shorthorns, which were sold at his decease, and fetched the enormous average of over 530*l*. each; second only to the prices fetched by Lord Dunmore's Bates herd, which realised a few years before over 550*l*. per head. I attended the beloved squire's funeral about five years since at Amersham Church, and shall never forget the sympathy shown by the hundreds of tenants, friends, and others who followed the brake containing the coffin, which was covered with flowers, drawn by a pair of his carriage-horses, and driven by his coachman to the grave. Amongst those who followed was old Tom Wingfield, who had been huntsman to the squire and his father in the Bicester country for over fifty years. Tom was then eighty years of age, and was the receiver of a handsome pension for his services, and himself joined the majority about two years ago. While speaking of the Drakes of Amersham I am reminded of the now obsolete system of close boroughs, as they were called, the representation of which was in the hands of one or perhaps two patrons, who, without consulting the wishes of the electors, sent down their own nominee, or nominated themselves, and thus entered the House of Commons without much expense or trouble. Terribly against modern ideas as this system is, it was not without its advantages, as it enabled rising young men of talent to find an opening into political life which might otherwise have been denied them. It was well known that the Drakes were not to be bought by any minister for the past hundred years, and no more independent members entered the House of Commons in the close borough days than Thomas Tyrwhitt Drake, the squire of the parish, and his brother Colonel Drake, who fought gallantly at Waterloo in the 'Blues.'

The little pocket borough of Wendover, only ten miles off, belonged to the Smiths, and was quite as remarkable for the independence of its representatives as its neighbour. As a corroboration of my views, this little borough, in its time, returned to Parliament John Hampden, the great patriot, Edmund Burke, William Pitt, and, I believe, Canning, a record, I think, of which many a newly enfranchised borough in the populous North of England might be proud.

It is an extraordinary circumstance, and an instance of what parliamentary customs were in the early days of representation, that but one side of the long main street of Amersham was in the borough, and this only up to a spot near the top of the town, where to this day there is an opening of about a foot between two houses, which marks the boundary. Some two centuries back the inhabitants of the one side of the street petitioned to be exempted from voting as they were poor, and could not afford to pay the expenses of their member to Parliament. This would seem to show that in early days members *were paid* for their services. So much for the ancient borough of Agmondesham : a dear, delightful specimen of an ancient, decayed market town, a fine old market house and hall over it, wide open street, and grand church, the glories of which place may possibly again arise, as the Metropolitan Railway is now opened to the town, and it will not be long before the Manchester, Sheffield, and Lincolnshire line will travel over it.

Since writing these records I have seen reviews of a most interesting work by the late Lady Verney (sister of the saintly Miss Florence Nightingale), who has written an account of some valuable documents relating to the Verney family, discovered at Claydon House, the residence of the venerable Sir Harry Verney, in which she alludes to the sad vicissitudes of the family towards the end of the eighteenth century. Lord Verney, who then resided at Claydon, fought a desperate contest for the representation of Bucks at the general election in 1784. This was considered at the time as one of the most important of the contests then raging throughout the kingdom. The candidates were Sir John Aubrey, the Hon. T. Grenville, both already mentioned in my former work, and Lord Verney. The poll lasted the full legal time of fourteen days, and my father had an old printed document of the time, giving the state of the poll at the termination in each hundred of the county, with the number of *plumpers*, or single votes, polled for each candidate, and the split votes divided between them. My father had heard from old people, resident in Aylesbury at the time, many curious stories of the manner in which this contest was carried on, and the acrimony shown by each party to the other. It appeared that Lord Verney was the independent and popular candidate, and every means were taken to lower him in the eyes of the electors, and during the poll a portion of the furniture was brought from Claydon House and publicly sold by auction, under the order of the sheriff, on the market hill of the town. The most-remarkable fact was, however, the cause of his lordship's defeat. Up to the last day of the poll it was uncertain which way the Ashridge or Bridgewater tenantry would poll, and it was at last decided that they should vote against Lord Verney.

It is necessary that my readers should understand that at that time, when the constituency of any borough or county could not poll one vote an hour, the poll was considered closed. On the last day Lord Verney was somewhere about thirty votes ahead of Aubrey, and the roads were so bad from the Ivinghoe or Ashridge district that the voters could not make their way to Aylesbury without great difficulty; and about eleven o'clock in the morning the Verney committee, sitting at the Bull's Head Inn, found their man was safe, as there was only another quarter of an hour left for the hour to be up when the poll was to be closed, and they had discovered that the Ashridge contingent could not arrive before twelve or one o'clock. While they were congratulating themselves on their certain success, a violent supporter of the party, who was their agent for the Buckingham division of the county, galloped into the town, rushed to the hustings, recorded his vote for 'Verney,' and hurried at once to the committee-room, and with great glee told his friends that 'he had just given a plumper for my lord.' 'By God, sir,' exclaimed the chairman of the committee, 'then you have lost our election!' and sure enough it did, as it kept the poll open another hour, which gave the Ashridge tenantry time to arrive, and Lord Verney lost the election by twenty-four votes, and this from the over-wrought zeal of a partisan who ought to have reported himself to the committee before he had been to poll. This circumstance added greatly to the chagrin and disappointment of the Verney party, and hastened the sad catastrophe which shortly afterwards overcame the family. The following was the state of the poll :—The Hon. T. Grenville, 2,264; Sir John Aubrey, 1,740; Lord Verney, 1,716; majority 24 only. The poll began on Wednesday, April 21, and ended on May 6, lasting, with the nomination, sixteen days.

CHAPTER II

Camden Neild—His gift to the Queen—A Welsh coal-owner and ironmaster—Bernal Osborne—Mentmore—'Conticuere omnes'—Kerry cattle—An Irish tale of a fox—Mrs. S. C. Hall's story—Lord Charles Russell, Mr. Perkins, and M.C.C. and W. G. Grace.

FOR many years I was much interested in seeing the arrival of a once noted character, and a visitor to the White Hart, in the person of Mr. Camden Neild. He was a barrister, and resided in lodgings with an old housekeeper in Cheyne Walk, Chelsea. He was of good family and a wretched miser. It is often said that an avaricious man cannot be an honest one, and this I believe to be true of him. I often remember his coming down, even in the winter, sitting on the knifeboard of Jem Wyatt's coach from London without a greatcoat or wrapper. His dress consisted generally of tight pantaloons—very much worn at the knees—Hessian boots, a threadbare blue coat with brass buttons, dirty buff waistcoat, high shirt-collar, large frill hanging out from his waistcoat, and a much-worn, old, low-crowned beaver hat. He had considerable landed property in the neighbourhood of Aylesbury, and would call at his tenant's, Johnny Horwood, of Buckland, near Tring, who held one of his farms of two hundred acres, and give Mrs. Horwood twopence to boil him two eggs, and buy a penny roll, and these he ate as he walked along the road in order to save breakfasting at an inn. He would then walk five miles to Aylesbury and stay at the White Hart, where he would order cold beef, &c., for luncheon. On one occasion the waiter, coming unexpectedly into the room, found he had cut two large slices of bread, and had laid between them two thick slices of beef, and pocketed them, thus saving a dinner. He was charged an extra shilling for it, which he most reluctantly paid. He would then walk on to North Marston, where he had a large property, a distance of eight miles. He never spent a shilling on his farms, and exacted the utmost farthing of rent. On one occasion he was found hanging by the neck in an outhouse by one of his tenants, who cut him down and saved his life, for which service he gave his deliverer a small reward.

At his death, to the surprise of everyone, he left the whole of his great wealth to the Queen, consisting of large landed estates and more than two hundred and fifty thousand pounds in cash. It was much regretted at the time that the advisers of Her Majesty sold the whole of the landed property, and thus prevented great improvements which would doubtless have been carried out. The Queen restored the chancel of North Marston Church, a rare specimen of the finest period of Perpendicular Gothic, and erected a stained glass window to Mr. Camden Neild's memory. Mr. Neild had put his name down for a subscription of 300*l*. to the Bucks Infirmary when it was first founded, but had never paid the money. Her Majesty at his decease paid the amount. This was another instance of his tenacity in clinging to his money, which was his GOD.

The foregoing traits remind me of a capital story I was told by a gentleman largely connected with the South Wales coal and iron industry. When old Mr. ——, who was enormously wealthy, was on his death-bed, a few hours before he breathed his last he sent for his managing agent, who had served him faithfully for many years, and, after a sad leave-taking, he said: 'My time is nearly come, and I wished to remind you that when I attended our board meeting last week I didn't take my fee; please see that it is paid.' His agent begged him not to let that matter at his last moments trouble him, and that he would see to it. After shaking hands, and saying 'God bless you,' and wishing him a last farewell, the agent was leaving the room, when the dying man faintly called him back, and said, 'You don't happen to have a guinea in your pocket, do you? because if you pay it now it will save a deal of trouble afterwards, and be more businesslike.' His agent had not the desired coin, and left the room, leaving his sordid master bereft of his fee. He died about three hours after, bequeathing to his family over two millions of money.

I have had the pleasure more than once of meeting Mr. Bernal Osborne, and a more delightful companion I never was acquainted with. I was accustomed to correspond with him at Newtown Anner, in Ireland, and have sent him choice specimens of exhibition poultry. On one occasion the late Baron Meyer de Rothschild invited me to Mentmore to meet him and some other friends, to talk about agriculture. Some little time previously Mr. Bernal Osborne had sent over to the Baron a lot of Irish cattle, which he called 'Kerries'; and one of the chief reasons for our visit was to see these specimens. Accordingly, I rode over from Aylesbury, about eight miles, and on my arrival found the party ready to start. The Baron and Mr. Bernal Osborne were on horseback, and there were two or three open carriages, one of which I was to drive, and amongst my companions was Lord Charles Russell, a veteran sportsman and a most courteous and agreeable gentleman. Before starting, the Baron called me aside, and wished me to get 'a rise' out of the distinguished Irishman by finding all the fault I could with these animals. After riding through a portion of the park, and admiring some very good grazing animals, we came to these Irish importations, and I certainly never saw more miserable, undersized creatures. I began by asking what they were, and was informed they were high-class graziers sent over by Mr. Osborne to show what could be done against English-bred ones; and that gentleman rode amongst them, pointing out what he considered their beauties and good qualities. I replied that they were not fit to go on to the most out-of-the-way village common in England, and utterly unfit for a gentleman's park. I said they reminded me of the Irish schoolmaster who began translating to his scholars the second Æneid of Virgil: '*Conticuere omnes*' ('They were all County Kerry men'). This raised a laugh, and Mr. Bernal Osborne reminded me of the continuation—'*intentique ora tenebant*' ('and they stood with their mouths wide open '). '*Obstupui*' ('I was bothered'), '*steteruntque comæ*' ('and my hair stood on end like bristles on the back of a fighting pig'), '*et vox faucibus hæsit*' ('and the divil of a word could I say'). We returned again to our Kerries, and I heard they had cost, with carriage by rail and all expenses paid *viâ* London and North-Western Railway to the neighbouring station at Cheddington, 6*l*. each, and that in the autumn, when they had put some flesh on their bones, they would make about 9*l*. to 10*l*. to the butcher. But the Baron had bought them more for his own household consumption than for the public, as they only came to about forty to forty-five stone of eight pounds each. They were of all colours, and very different to the Kerries now in use as dairy cattle, which are all black in colour and much larger, and are most excellent milk and cream producers, and more suitable, in my opinion, for most districts than Jerseys. The Kerries are much hardier, and give on the whole a greater quantity of milk, and are now so highly thought of that the Royal Agricultural Society gives them a class to themselves at their show, with special prizes for the breed.

Mr. Bernal Osborne kept us in continued laughter by many Irish stories, told in a rich brogue, one of which I will try to remember:

A blacksmith, very early one morning, was going through a plantation leading to a gentleman's house to shoe some horses, and in the roadway a fox was sitting, with one fore-paw held up, his ears laid back, his brush draggled, and he did not move, but looked up beseechingly to the blacksmith. The blacksmith stooped down and looked at his foot, and found a swelling and gathering;

and he took a horse-nail from his box and pricked the part, and let the matter out. It gave the fox immediate relief, and he nodded his head and trotted off into the wood. Would you believe it?—the next morning when he went to open his door he found a couple of fine fat dead fowls laid there. The blacksmith took them inside, and the next morning there was a couple of good fat ducks, and begor, sor, this went on for some weeks, and one day there was a fine young goose. Well, sor, the last winter there was a farmer out with the hounds, and when the fox broke covert, it was this same fellow, and the farmer viewed him away, and gave the 'Tally ho!' and it was this man's hen roost that the fox went to each night, till he had cleared most of the poultry away, and this was how the fox got upside with his enemy.

This amusing story reminded me of, I think, one of Mrs. S. C. Hall's, who records that one night a fox entered the cabin of Tim Flanagan, and coolly sat down by the hot embers, lighted his pipe, and began smoking, as natural as any other man. Tim was telling this story to a gentleman who was incredulous, and expressed his doubts as to its truth, and when Tim said 'the fox then took up the newspaper and began reading it,' his listener could stand it no longer, and said, 'What should the fox want with reading the newspaper?' Tim replied, 'How the divil was he to tell where the hounds met if he didn't?' This was conclusive.

After a *recherché* luncheon I left Mentmore with pleasing recollections of my visit. I said above that Lord Charles Russell was one of our party, and this reminds me that one day I was going to London with my old friend Henry Perkins, secretary to the M.C.C., and at Cheddington we got into the same carriage with that veteran old cricketer, and in the course of conversation his lordship asked if they were not getting up a testimonial to W. G. Grace. Mr. Perkins replied that it was so, and that subscriptions were coming in in amounts varying from one to five guineas. Lord Charles then said, 'Well, W. G. has given me three times as much pleasure in watching his play as any other man I ever saw, so I will give you three times as much as anyone else. Put me down for fifteen.'

HAMPDEN HOUSE, THE SEAT OF THE EARL OF BUCKINGHAMSHIRE
(THE BIRTHPLACE OF THE PATRIOT HAMPDEN)

CHAPTER III

John Hampden—His death—Chalgrove Field—Exhumation of his body—Sacrilegious conduct of Lord Nugent and others—Desecration of the remains of the great patriot—Identification of his body—His portrait—Robertson, of Hampden Gardens—Jasper More—Visit to Roman Gravels mine—Address to the miners—Prizes for hillside allotments—Lord Clive—Emperor Hadrian's mine.

WHEN I was a boy at school, in the year 1830, the county of Bucks was agitated at what was considered a great act of sacrilege, viz. the exhumation of the body of the great patriot, John Hampden. John Hampden, as all who have studied the history of England know, was the patriot who identified himself with the cause of liberty, and opposed what he considered the arbitrary conduct of his sovereign, Charles I. When he learnt that Prince Rupert, who held Oxford with the Royalist forces, was harassing the country around Thame, which was situate about twelve miles from his residence at Great Hampden, he placed himself at the head of his troop of yeomanry, and, being joined with many others who leaned to the Parliamentary party, he marched out to meet the Royalists, and came in contact with them at Chalgrove Field, about three miles from Thame, on June 18, 1643, and after a sharp skirmish Hampden received his death wounds. Several accounts had been given of the nature and extent of the wounds, and Lord Nugent, being about to write a Life of Hampden, was desirous of getting hold of the real facts of the case, and conceived the reprehensible plan of exhuming the body, and thus endeavour to reconcile some of these contradictory statements. It was generally considered that two carbine balls struck him in the shoulder, which was fractured, that he fell on his horse's neck, and hung thereon, and managed to reach the town of Thame in great agony, that he rode into the yard of the Greyhound Inn, and that, being attended by a surgeon, he got worse and the next day died of lockjaw, to the great grief of the nation. Local tradition says a soldier of his own party accidentally shot him. Clarendon says, 'he was shot in the shoulder with a brace of bullets which brake the bone.' Hume says the same, as do also Lord Nugent and Guizot.

Another account is totally different, with which I unhesitatingly agree. In the Earl of Oxford's papers it says :—

> Two of the Hanleys and one of the Foleys being at supper with Sir Robert Pye, at Farringdon House, Berks, related the account of Hampden's death as follows :—' That at the action at

Chalgrove Field his pistol burst, and shattered his hand in a fearful manner. He, however, rode off, and got to his quarters; but finding the wound mortal, he sent for Sir Robert Pye, then a colonel in the Parliamentary army, who had married his eldest daughter, and told him he looked to him as in some degree accessory to his death, as the pistols were a present from him. Sir Robert assured him that he had bought them in Paris of an eminent maker, and that he had proved them himself. It appeared, on examining the other pistol, that it was loaded to the muzzle with several supernumerary charges, owing to the carelessness of a servant, who was ordered to see the pistols loaded every morning, which he did, without drawing the former charge.'

Other statements were made that he died at Thame of lockjaw. The body of the great patriot was carried from the little town to Great Hampden Church, escorted and followed to his grave by his yeoman tenants and their sorrowing neighbours. Some years ago I saw on the walls of the Academy a picture, I think by Calderon, of the melancholy *cortège* passing through the Beech Woods on the Chilterns to his last resting-place in the church adjoining the mansion. He was buried alongside of his first wife, where his ancestors had been buried for many generations. I now have to record what I remember to have heard of the shameful act of sacrilege and the indecent proceedings which were carried out with a view to discover the body of Hampden, and to verify the cause of his death. It appears that in 1828 a most remarkable scene was enacted in Great Hampden Church, said to have been sanctioned by the then Earl of Buckinghamshire, the patron of the living, himself a descendant of the patriot and owner and occupier of Hampden House. Lord Nugent, then M.P. for the borough and hundreds of Aylesbury, Hampden being a village within the

hundreds, obtained the consent of the incumbent, the Rev. G. W. Brooks, and excused himself for the sacrilegious act of exhuming the body on the ground of clearing up historical doubts; but the disgraceful manner in which the act was performed was told to me, and had been placed on record by an eye-witness. The search took place on July 21, by Lord Nugent and Mr. Counsellor (afterwards Lord) Denman, the Rev. G. W. Brooks, and about twenty onlookers and assistants. Several leaden coffins were examined, and at last the plate of one was examined, but it was so corroded that it broke into small pieces on being touched. The coffin had originally been enclosed in wood, covered in velvet, a small portion only of which was apparent; they were then nearly certain that this was the one they were in quest of. The parish plumber descended into the vault and commenced cutting *across* the coffin, then *longitudinally*, until the whole was sufficiently loosened to be rolled back, in order to lift up the wooden lid beneath. Under this was another lid, both in good preservation. It was found that the coffin had originally been filled with sawdust, and when removed, the process of examination commenced. My old friend, the late Mr. R. Gibbs, says:—

Silence reigned. Not a whisper or a breath was heard. Each present awaited the result, as to what appearance the face would present when uncovered. Lord Nugent descended into the grave, and first removed the outer cloth, which was firmly wrapped round the body, then a second, then a third, great care having been taken to preserve the body. Here a very singular scene presented itself. No regular features were apparent, although the face retained a death-like whiteness, and showed the various windings of the veins and blood-vessels beneath the skin. The upper row of teeth was

DESECRATION OF HAMPDEN'S BODY

perfect and was quite sound. A little beard remained on the chin, the whiskers were strong, and the hair was a full auburn brown. The eyes were slightly sunk in, and were covered by the same white film as the face. They then raised up the coffin altogether, and placed it in the centre of the church. Being placed on a tressle, the first operation was to examine the arms, which nearly retained their original size. *On lifting up the right arm, we found it was dispossessed of a hand.* It was then conjectured that it was amputated. On searching under the cloths *we found the hand*, or rather a number of small bones, enclosed in a separate cloth, for about six inches up the arm the flesh had wasted away, evidently smaller than the left arm, to which the hand was firmly united, and which presented no symptom of decay. *Even the nails remained entire.* We thought it unnecessary to examine further, as this striking coincidence of the loss of the right hand would justify the belief that Sir R. Pye's statement was correct. They then examined the right shoulder. *The clavicle was firmly united to the scapula, and no appearance of any wound ever having been inflicted.* On the contrary, the left shoulder was smaller and sunken in.

I heard that then Lord Nugent gashed the flesh in a most unseemly manner with a penknife, and tried to remove the arms—and the socket of the right arm was perfectly white and healthy, with no appearance of a wound. The left arm, on the contrary, was of a brownish cast, and the clavicle quite loose, and it had evidently been dislocated. In order to examine the head and hair the body was raised up, *and supported by a shovel.* On removing the cloths, which adhered firmly to the back of the head, they found the hair in a complete state of preservation. It was of a dark auburn colour, and, according to the custom of the times, was very long, from five to six inches. It was drawn up and tied at the top of the head with black silk. The ends had the appearance of being cut off. Some doubts had been expressed as to this being the body of Hampden, but the fact of the body being found next that of his wife, and being buried in the chancel, in cerecloth, and in lead and wooden coffins, shows it must have been a person of eminence.

I now come to the most extraordinary part of my story, which was told me by the late Rev. W. E. Partridge, the rector of the parish of Horsenden, about three miles from Hampden. The story had been told him by a highly respectable and truthful man, Mr. Robertson, whom I well remember. He was head gardener at Hampden House, and was also a confidential servant to the Earl of Buckinghamshire. Robertson stated that

he was present at the exhumation, and that there was no really authentic portrait known of the great patriot, and that a search was being made amongst some old portraits and lumber in the attics, when he saw a portrait that seemed to be looking at him, a sight he should never forget as long as he lived. He immediately recognised it as the face and figure of the man he had seen in the grave at Hampden Church. On the arrival home of his master from France he told him of his impression, and while examining the picture they removed a piece of old canvas, and, to the great joy of the Earl and himself, they found the patriot's name written very legibly, and a statement that it had been presented by one of the Bedford family. It ran thus: 'John Hampden, 1640; a present to Sir Wm. Russell, and afterwards given to Lord John Russell.'

It was noticed by many present at the sacrilegious act, that the face was in good preservation, but that on exposure to the air it began to disappear. Mr. Grace, whom I knew well, and who was present, says that the eyebrows were perfect and he could quite discern the expression of the face, and he thought it a beautiful *dead* face. So disgracefully was the whole thing managed that the body was left uncared for in the parish church the whole of the next day, and exposed to the gaze of anyone who came from idle curiosity to see it. And this was the insult offered to the dead body of one of the greatest men England ever produced, whose life and death made a mark in English history which will never be effaced. It has been said by many writers of eminence, and I myself believe it to be true, that if Hampden had lived it is probable that his loyalty and patriotism would have been able to prevent the catastrophe which the country had to deplore, the murder of their king.

The family of Hampden were a great family for many centuries; the well-known couplet quoted by Sir Walter Scott in 'Ivanhoe' is typical of their importance :

> Tring, Wing, and Ivinghoe,
> Three churches all of a row ;
> These three Hampden did foregoe
> For striking of the Black Prince a blow,
> And glad he did escape so.

Hampden House stands on the summit of the Chiltern Hills, and is about three miles from Princes Risborough, which was the residence of the Black Prince, and it is not unlikely that, during some altercation between the two, high words might have been used, and the lordly Hampden could not restrain himself, and in the heat of dispute thoughtlessly struck the prince ; but there is no authentic record of it.

In one of Black's most delightful novels, ' Kilmeny,' he describes most vividly Hampden and its umbrageous surroundings, and his heroine is mentioned as Miss Burnham, and the spot also is called Burnham. It is evident, however, that it was Hampden that was meant, and the glade, about a mile long, stretches down the hill from the mansion to Havenfield, where the mad infidel inhabitant of the house resided, by name a Major Backhouse; and I well remember, as a boy, having his tomb pointed out to me in the corner of a field where he had insisted on being

OLD ENTRANCE LODGES AND QUEEN'S GAP AT HAMPDEN

buried. He lay there for some years, and was then exhumed and buried in Great Missenden Churchyard. A story of singular interest is told of this open glade or avenue in front of Hampden. It is said that Queen Elizabeth, on her visit to the grandfather of the patriot, was shown to her bedchamber by Mr. Hampden, and on looking from the window she was much struck with the grandeur of the timber and the sylvan beauty of the landscape, and said: 'Don't you think, Mr. Hampden, if you had an avenue opening down the hill it would be an improvement?' In this opinion her host acquiesced. The next morning, on looking from her window, the queen saw that the avenue was formed and scores of noble trees lay on the hillside! This showed the power of the then owner over so large a number of retainers as to be able to accomplish so great a work in a single night. The avenue is still called 'The Queen's Gap,' and I have a general belief that the story is in the main true. The patriot Hampden was returned to Parliament, first for the little borough of Wendover, about three miles distant, afterwards disfranchised by the Reform Bill of 1832, and subsequently he sat for the county of Bucks till the time of his death. His name is still revered amongst the inhabitants of the district, as it is also by every student of English history, as one of the noblest characters that ever lived. His name and residence give another instance of the truth of Lord Beaconsfield's remark, when he spoke of the 'great historic county of Bucks.'

It has been my privilege for some years past to enjoy the friendship of Mr. Jasper More, M.P. for one of the divisions of Shropshire. For some time I had given the subject of village clubs some attention, and was conversant with the system successfully carried out at Tyler's Green, Penn, Bucks. Accordingly Mr. More invited me to come on a visit to his charming residence, Linley Hall, near Bishop's Castle, with the object of meeting the miners and other labourers, and explaining to them the advantages of co-operation in this most desirable object. Mr. More some two or three years before had determined to try the experiment of cultivating by allotments a large portion of the hillsides adjoining his mines; one of these was the 'Roman Gravels,' of which I shall speak farther on. These hillsides had been almost useless, but his practical mind suggested to him that he might make a small rental from the surface, find employment for the miners at their leisure hours, and give the men an interest in the soil and a knowledge of agricultural operations. Mr. More therefore divided a moderately large acreage into allotments of from a rood to eight or ten acres, according to the wishes of the tenants, and I think at a rental of five shillings a rood, or quarter of an acre, to about one pound an acre, all rates and outgoings being paid by the owner. He then offered prizes for the produce of this land, and the same for the best cultivated portions. I had the honour of being invited the following autumn to come down and judge for the prizes, and at the same time to address the miners on the great advantages to them in the establishment of the club, where they could get reasonable refreshment at moderate charges, and a good reading-room, bagatelle-board, and other amusements. At a certain hour it had been arranged that I should address them, and preparations had been made for the presence of reporters, and also for Mrs. More with other friends. It was a novel, and to me most curious sight to see the men emerge from the mine, in their rough and dirty mining dresses, with candles stuck into the brims of their hats, and the usual mining appliances.

I believe there were nearly three hundred of them, and a most attentive and interested audience I had. I dilated on the club advantages, and explained to them the best systems of cultivation of their various crops, and the necessity of cleanliness of cultivation, and the proper routine of cropping. Several of the men stepped forward and made many very sensible remarks, and questioned me on those subjects relating to the cultivation of their allotments. The next day I examined the crops and awarded a considerable number of prizes, which Mr. More, with great discrimination, offered in the shape of various manures and farm seeds, not only to benefit the tenants pecuniarily, but to show them the advantages of guano, superphosphate, nitrate, &c. I believe the plan is still in existence and is very successful. It was one of the most interesting meetings I ever addressed. The mine was called the 'Roman Gravels' from a pig of lead having been found some years since in the *débris* near the entrance of the mine, with 'Hadrianus Imperator' inscribed and cast upon it. With my visit to the former residence of the great Lord Clive my journey to Mr. More and his hospitable home ended, and I may truly say it was a *red letter* day in my agricultural career.

CHAPTER IV

Volunteers—Amersham Yeoman—Anecdote of a solicitor—Sporting customs of gormandising—Amersham v. Beaconsfield—Parish rivalries—Boiled beef and concomitants—Vinegar—Triumphant return home—Prize fight between Tom Hatton and Mickey Gannon—The Archdeacon's opinions—Jem Mace, Champion of England—London and North-Western Railway—Anecdote of tenant of Denbigh Hall—Prevention of an accident—A visit to Hughenden—A wreath on the great statesman's grave—The visit of the Queen—The casket placed on his tomb—And final closing of tomb—Anecdote of Devonshire rector—The 'Saddling Bell'—A Northumberland rector's ride to church—Sports of the field at Oxford—An Oxford undergraduate is plucked in his divinity—The 'Pluck' coach.

THERE are many good stories which have been often told, but less often recorded in print. Whilst eulogising the volunteer movement, we are apt to forget that during the great Revolutionary war with France, in the beginning of the present century, most of the great towns had their armed or trained bands, and made a goodly show; and it was thought to be a grand idea of William Pitt's to establish these volunteers, and especially in the metropolis, where he thought it necessary not only for the defence of the empire, but to engraft the disaffected amongst the well-disposed, and thus render them useless for evil. A good story is told of the great Commoner, that one of the City companies, fired with military patriotism, had raised a band of volunteers and waited on William Pitt, and in their address they stipulated that 'they were not to be sent out of the country.' Pitt said they had made an omission,—' Except in case of invasion.'

My father used to tell a good story of a young solicitor in the town of Amersham who was on his way to Chorleywood Common to drill as a mounted yeoman. When he had gone about three miles, he saw an old-fashioned farmer in a field, and as he rode by he made a great noise by drawing his sword with a crash from his scabbard, and flourishing it round his head, shouted out, ' Hallo! my good man, have you seen anything of the French about here?' 'Noa,' he said, ' I ha'n't; *if I had I shouldn't have seen you here.*'

A gross form of personal rivalry some years since consisted in eating or drinking a certain amount of food or beer, either within a fixed time or by performing against each other; and I have heard there were two noted eaters of boiled beef residing, one at Beaconsfield and the other at Amersham. A match was made between them which was to come off at the former town. The beef was dressed with the usual concomitants of boiled turnips, carrots, and other vegetables, and great excitement ensued, and in the evening the inhabitants of Amersham were on the *qui vive* for the news of their champion. At last their representative appeared in a gig, the horse decorated, and himself with blue ribbons, and on being asked ' how he got on,' the winner, in accents of contempt, answered, ' *Why, I bate him afore I got to winegar.*' It appeared that when this worthy got to ' winegar ' he never did leave off.

Towards the last few years of my farming career I had seen the evils of giving almost unlimited beer at hay and corn harvest, and was determined to try and put a stop to the inordinate amount consumed. Accordingly, a week or two before corn harvest, I called my men together and expatiated on the folly of their drinking so much beer, and added that I would give them sixteen shillings per acre to cut, carry, stack, and thatch all the corn, about 120 acres, and would find reaping machine, horses, carts, &c. In addition I was to do the raking up, *and they were to find their own beer.* To this they cordially agreed, and I impressed on them that they ought only to drink what was necessary for them. That same evening their foreman, at their request, went off to the local brewery and ordered '*four hundred*' gallons of beer! When I heard of it and remonstrated, I am sorry to say that they justified it, and said it was only about three gallons of beer to the acre! After this what is to be done? Let teetotallers remonstrate, and teach the working-classes better. I am bound to say I don't think I saw any of them drunk; perhaps the beer was too attenuated.

I was one day going to London, and had heard that a prize-fight was to come off between 'Tom Hatton' and 'Micky Gannon,' two noted bruisers, for 50*l.* a side, and that the contest was to come off at 'Marston Gate,' a small station about half-way between Aylesbury and Cheddington Junction. This place had been more than once selected for these contests, because there was a field adjoining the station which was half in Bucks and the other half in Herts, and about two miles distant was the county of Beds, so that if the county police intervened the company could retire into an adjoining county, and so evade the law. When the train arrived, a whole host got into the carriages, it was about 8.30 A.M., and amongst them two heavily damaged specimens of humanity, carefully wrapped up in horse-cloths. On arriving at Cheddington all had to change carriages, and wait for the up train. From one of them alighted my worthy vicar, the Archdeacon of Buckingham, the Rev. E. Bickersteth, late Dean of Lichfield. He and I were walking up and down the platform, and took great notice of our fellow-passengers, who were seated on some benches waiting for the train. The two principals were seated there with frightfully swollen faces, eyes bunged up, distorted noses, and puffy cheeks, black, blue, and yellow, and one man with his arm in a sling. The shocked ecclesiastic, after passing them and noticing them, said, 'Mr. Fowler, those are very singular-looking men ; there are two poor fellows much injured ; *has there been a railway accident?*' I was much amused, and replied, ' No, Mr. Archdeacon, both those poor men's faces accidentally came in contact with each other's fists, and hence their sad appearance ; to be plain, there has been a prize-fight, and they are the combatants, and those around are their backers.' ' Indeed!' he said, ' this is very interesting ; they seem very kind to each other. Who is that big, rather good-looking man, helping them most carefully and kindly into that first-class carriage ? ' ' That, sir,' I said, ' is the champion of England.' ' Indeed! what, Dymoke of Scrivelsby ?' ' No,' I replied ; ' the one is a champion of peace, the other of pugilistic warfare ; that is "Jem

Mace," the well-known champion of the prize-ring.' I never saw the little Archdeacon more astonished, and he told me afterwards that he was surprised at the kindness and attention shown to the combatants.

When the London and North-Western Railway was first opened it ran to Box Moor, and some weeks after to Tring station, and later on to Bletchley. The next move was from the Birmingham end to Rugby, and then to Roade and Blisworth, and Messrs. Chaplin and Horne filled up the connecting link from thence to Bletchley by omnibus. There was a farmhouse within about a mile of that place called Denbigh Hall, tenanted by an old friend of mine, and when the line was opened to its full length, from Birmingham to London, he could hear the mail train rushing past about three o'clock every morning, and had become so perfectly accustomed to it that he could sleep on soundly without being aroused. One night he woke up because he had *not* heard it go past, and he lay awake for some time, till at last he became alarmed, and arose and woke up the stationmaster, who was in bed, as the train was not timed to stop at Bletchley. He found out from the man on duty that it had not passed, so he signalled back, and sent on to Blisworth and found an accident had occurred; and, as there were no telegraph signals at that time, he sent back towards Leighton Buzzard and stopped the down train, and by that means averted a severe collision which would undoubtedly have occurred. Here was a curious instance of an accident being prevented because a man did *not* hear the train go by.

My daughter sent me an account of a visit she paid

to Hughenden, a short time after the burial of the Earl of Beaconsfield, which has some points of considerable interest, and, I think, not generally known. She was staying with a married sister at Great Marlow, and they were desirous of putting a wreath of primroses and violets on the tomb of the great statesman. They drove to High Wycombe by the picturesque villages of Wooburn Green and Wycombe Marsh, and thence walked to Hughenden. On asking the way from a pedestrian whom they met, he told them that the Queen was at the church, and that she had come to visit the tomb of Lord Beaconsfield, and to put a wreath on it. They hurried up the hill, and found she had left the grave and gone to the manor.

Fortunately (my daughter writes) we found no one in the church but a policeman, and some workmen busily building up the grave. We asked if we might put our wreath on the railing round it, but were told it was impossible without the vicar's permission. With feelings of deep despair (she goes on to say) we stood looking into the vault, where the coffin of the late Earl lay, quite visible, and covered with flowers, with the wreath just brought by the Queen resting above all; on either side were the coffins of Lady Beaconsfield and Mr. James Disraeli, his brother, as also Miss Williams, the faded flowers on the former being quite visible, as also the new wreath sent by Lady Burdett-Coutts. To our relief we met the rector, the Rev. Mr. Blagden, who, with great courtesy, asked us to return with him to the grave, where he permitted us to hang our wreath upon the railings, kindly suggesting we should put ours on the point next to the one on which the Queen's primrose wreath was hanging. With trembling but grateful hands it was placed where the vicar proposed, and after thanking him for his kindness we turned to leave, when he asked us if we would like to see the contents of a little box which he carried concealed beneath his coat. He then produced a casket, containing a portrait of the late Earl, which he was taking to place on the coffin, after the Queen had seen it, and which had not been put there, as stated in the papers, on the day of the funeral. The vicar placed the casket in our hands, and after we had examined it we returned it to him, and he at once proceeded to dispose of it as he had told us. Thus the visit proved to be a never-forgotten day to us, and we waited to see the last of the sacred casket and the coffin of the mighty dead till it was hidden by the bricklayers, never again perhaps to be opened or seen by human eye.[1]

'From grave to gay, from lively to severe.' When the 'Varsity men were accustomed to ride their 'aristocratic' races over my farm there were two sportsmen pre-eminent among them. Their names were then well known in their respective colleges, but it would be wise now to suppress them, as one is a learned recorder of a populous northern town, and the other a worthy rector of a parish in Devonshire. The former was on a visit at the latter's rectory, and one Sunday morning at breakfast they were rather late; the little 'tinkling' bell that usually rings five minutes before the service commences had begun to peal. The rector jumped up from the table and rang for his valet. When he came into the room the rector said, 'Come, John, don't you hear *the saddling bell? Bring the colours.*' The domestic hurried away, fetched the surplice, and put it on his master's shoulders, who then in good time entered the church and began the service.

I heard also another good story of a sporting rector in the extreme north, who was *facile princeps* as a rider over our Aylesbury course, and who won more races as an undergraduate than any other at the 'Varsity.

[1] I ought to have said that the casket which contained the portrait was long in the possession of the Disraeli family, and was two and a half pounds in weight.

Amongst his sporting parishioners his horsemanship was greatly admired. His rectory-house was on a hill about a mile distant from the church, which was also on another hill with a valley between them. The rector often rode to church, sometimes across country, putting his horse up at one of the farmers' stables near the church, and the parishioners assembled in the churchyard, waiting for his advent, would watch his progress from the rectory with keen relish, expressing themselves enthusiastically as one fence after the other was safely negotiated. One of them would say, ' He's safely over the single ; ' another, ' Now he's at the double ;' ' Yes, he's all right ;' ' What will he do at the rails?' ' He's well over ; ' and the last thing he jumped was the churchyard wall, saving his time by three minutes. I am writing these anecdotes with no irreverent spirit, as I am told there are no more devoted men to the wants of their poorer parishioners than these very men, and they are no mean preachers from their pulpits. I never could see why exercise on horseback and the reasonable sports of the field should be loudly condemned, any more than exercise on the river or the cricket-field. Muscular Christianity is human and full of good omen, and oftentimes unites the parson and his flock. These reminiscences, it must not be forgotten, are of events nearly forty years ago. I can remember a story being told, when I was a boy, of a clergyman I well knew, who was the son of an old-fashioned baronet. The aspirant to Holy Orders was plucked at college in his divinity. On being asked ' Who was the mediator between God and man?' he replied at once, with much complacency, 'The Archbishop of Canterbury.' But this man was pushed through his examination after that, so as to enable him to have his father's living of his native parish, and was anything but a fair specimen of the rural clergy. I have often wondered how the people put up with the scandalous system of pluralities in the church at the time I was a boy. Amongst my recollections of country clerical life I have been much amused at the following rural anecdote. It is, however, necessary to explain that, until a few years ago, nearly every farmer, and even other householders, in the country brewed their own beer, and much rivalry existed as to which house should brew the best. The October brewing was generally considered fit for consumption in the January or February following, and the March brewing was fit for the summer and autumn use. Good beer was thought to be of good strength if it was brewed with eight bushels of malt to the hogshead of fifty-four imperial gallons; and after the 'first run,' as it was called, had been drawn off, more water was added, and the *table* beer was the produce. At an outlying village in Bucks, the rector, on a certain Sunday, on preaching his sermon, gave out the text 'First *Hebrews*, 9 and 10,' whereupon an old-fashioned farmer, renowned for a good tap, called out, ' And wery pretty tipple too; *I brews* eight!' He explained to the rector after church that he meant eight bushels to the hogshead. The worthy rector, to enable him to test the quality, called on him a few days afterwards, and pronounced the brewing excellent, and explained his text more fully and, it is hoped, satisfactorily.

CHAPTER V

Restoration of chancel in Aylesbury Church—A rector's economical suggestion of a slated roof—Prebend of Lincoln—Steeplechasing—The old Broughton country—Jem Mason and William Archer—'Varsity riders in the 'Fifties'—A dead heat and heavy stakes with Tom Price and Ned Enoch—Charlie and George Symonds—Joe Tollit—Perrin's old horse Phœnix—The Pratt Club—And Grand National Hunt Steeplechases—Over Prebendal Farm—Lowlander's first appearance—And after performances.

MY father had been vicar's churchwarden for more than twenty-five years, and the fine old parish church at Aylesbury had fallen into a sad state of decay, but the state of the chancel was simply disgraceful. It was very large, and a fine specimen of pure Early English architecture. This chancel was, of course, the property of the rector, who was oftentimes a layman, but in this case was a prebend of Lincoln, and my farm, at a rental of over 500*l.* per annum, was attached to this prebend, for which no service whatever was performed; it was simply a disgraceful sinecure. The Bishop of Lincoln, Pretyman Tomline, used to put all his sons, nephews, nieces' husbands, and every relative of his family into all the fat livings of his diocese, many of them holding two or three incumbencies, and it was one of this family that became Prebend of Aylesbury. My father wrote to him saying he must come up at once, and arrange for the repair and restoration of this chancel, as the parishioners were about to repair the church. The worthy prebend was a rector of a parish in the north of Bucks, and came to see the state of his chancel. He called on my father, and said he thought he could easily arrange for its repair—especially the roof, which was covered with very thick ancient lead of four hundred years' standing. He said, 'I think if we took off the lead, and mended the rafters—and then *neatly slated it*—it would do very well!' My father most indignantly remarked, 'Yes, sir, and by sale of the lead put at least 300*l*. into your pocket. No; you may depend on it where I find lead there shall be lead, where I find oak it shall be oak, and where stone it shall be stone. I'll have no work scamped here. Hundreds of parish churches have been served as you propose; the lead sacrilegiously removed for tiles and slates, and stucco and rough-cast for stone or flint.' The rector found he had caught a Tartar, and reluctantly consented to do what was necessary. To complete the work cost about 300*l*., and when he came to settle the bills he said, 'It is very hard on me to have to pay this, for you will scarcely believe it, but this is the *third* chancel I have had to repair this year!'

I had been for several years connected with steeplechasing, and the old Broughton country, as it was called, over my father's farm was a most severe course, and had been made memorable by several historical contests, more especially by the celebrated race between The British Yeoman, ridden by Jem Mason, and Vain Hope, ridden by W. Archer, the father of the celebrated flat-race jockey, Fred Archer. In the present day this course would be pronounced absolutely impracticable. There were some enormous doubles, and the 'Bullfinchers' had to be negotiated uncut, and if relaid as a 'stake and bounder' were so strong that, unless a horse cleared the bramble binder, it was almost sure to throw him down. The Brook was a mill-stream forming the mill-head and was approached up-hill, and although not very wide was very deep, and the landing was on a descent of about four feet ; in fact, it was a trap, and unless the horse was held pretty tightly in hand, and ridden with a cool determination, there was either a refusal or a jump too short, and the gallant steed and rider came to grief. The consequence was that, even in a field of fifteen or sixteen horses at the post, it was rarely that more than five or six were seen at the finish. I admit this tested most severely a really first-class hunter, but it was unsatisfactory to the onlookers, who like to see a close finish. The 'Varsity riders from Oxford were on the whole well pleased with this course, and the riders of that period, many of whom I am most pleased to record are still hale and hearty, were such hard riders as Lord Cork, then Lord Dungarvan, Lord Coventry, Colonel Blundell, Messrs. Burton, Dewar, Goldingham, Rev. James Allgood, Messrs. W. Beach, M.P., A. Peel, W. Jenkins, Sir Roger Palmer, W. Chaplin, and many others, whom I can scarcely remember now. This was in the early 'fifties.' The stakes were not very heavy, but the honour of special colleges was at stake, as also that of rival keepers of stables, such as old Charlie Symonds and his brother George, Joe Tollit and his brother George, yclept by the irreverent 'Beelzebub,' and old Perrin. This rivalry was considered sufficient inducement to bring out the greatest talent both of horse and man in that ancient and far-famed seat of learning. As an instance of this feeling, I remember an extraordinary race in 1853, in which seven horses ran. 'Old Tom Price,' often seen now (1893) on many race-courses,

THE DEAD HEAT
Mr. Geo. Symonds' Janus, ridden by Ned Enoch
Mr. Perrin's Phœnix, ridden by Tom Price

rode Perrin's Phœnix, and Ned Enoch, who I believe now trains for that prince of sportsmen, who I am sure will excuse me for calling him 'Jemmy Lowther,' rode a horse of George Symonds named Janus. These horses ran a dead heat, after going three and a half miles. The owners refused to divide the stakes, and for the honour of their respective stables resolved on running it over again, and in this final contest Janus won by a short length. My brother, Richard Fowler, was judge, and tells me how terribly distressed both horses and men were at the finish. To sum up all, *the value of the stakes was only 7l.*, and the second saved his stake. These horses and men were content to ride seven miles of frightfully difficult country for 1*l.* a mile! What a contrast to the great steeplechase stakes of this period!

In the year 1853 I entered on the tenancy of the Prebendal Farm at Aylesbury, and seeing what remarkable facilities there were on this farm for a first-class course, I commenced and completed the line which has now, for so many years, become renowned as the best *natural* course in England. There are two meetings of public importance that I think it right to mention as having been run over this line. The first was on April 4, 1859, when the late Duke of Sutherland, then Marquis of Stafford, Lord Burghersh, afterwards Earl of Westmorland, Mr. Lorraine Baldwin, a veteran sportsman of high standing and still living, with one or two others, came to consult me about holding the 'Pratt Club' Steeplechase. The preliminaries were soon settled, and the races came off with brilliant success. The first race was the Hunters' Stakes, and was won in gallant style by Lord Strathmore on his horse The Charm, Mr. Peach's Wellington second, and Lord Suffield's St. Lawrence, ridden by the owner, third. The next race was the Hack Stakes, won again by Lord Strathmore on The Tartar, the Earl of Stamford's Warrington second. Mr. George Drake, Sir M. Crofton, Colonel Forrester, and Mr. Leigh's names appeared among the winners of other races. Lord Strathmore was delighted with his success, and pronounced the line to be the finest he had ever ridden over. Perhaps the crowning honour was gained by this now well-known course when the Grand National Hunt Meeting was run over it on March 3 and 4, 1874. This was made specially memorable by the appearance in public, almost for the first time, of that celebrated race-horse Lowlander, who ran in a hurdle race, and was placed third. In June of the same year Lowlander won the Royal Hunt Cup at Ascot, nor did his successes end there, for he won several other good races during the year and remained unbeaten at the end of it. The Grand National Hunt race was won by Mr. Vyner's Lucellum, Mr. Archie Peel being second on Ballot Box: twelve started. Five other races, all well contested, were run that day; and the second day the Master of Hounds Steeplechase was won by Mr. F. Bennett's Miss Hungerford, Lord Willoughby de Broke's Abbess second, and Mr. Jem Hill's Glenlyon third. There were six other races, which made up a most successful meeting, and this was the only occasion on which this course was made a 'gate-money' meeting. Over 1,200*l.* was taken for gate, stand, and carriage inclosure. It is rather amusing to read the names of the stewards—President: H.R.H. the Prince of Wales. Stewards: the Duke of Buckingham, Benjamin Disraeli, M.P., S. G. Smith, M.P., Sir A. de Rothschild, Sir Philip Duncombe, Colonel Richardson Gardiner, and other 'grave and reverend signiors,' with such ardent sportsmen as Lords Jersey, Carrington, and Valentia, Sir Robert Harvey, M.P., Nathaniel and

Leopold de Rothschild, John Gerard Leigh, W. M. Wroughton, and others. These steeplechase meetings at Aylesbury, although shorn of their old associations, are still popular and attract a large concourse of visitors.

CHAPTER VI

Harry Poole—Count d'Orsay—Napoleon III.—Mr. Pennington, High Sheriff of Bucks—and the grand fête at Cherbourg—Lord Beaconsfield—' Lothair '—The FitzClarences—The King's—Mr. De Burgh's, and Rothschild's stag hounds—Cliveden—Duchess of Sutherland—Brahmin cow—Cattle show—Spring gardening—The Duchess and Fleming—Sewage irrigation—Maplin Sands—Prince Albert's plan—Mr. Yarrow—Peat charcoal—Osiers.

AMONG my hunting acquaintances was the late Harry Poole, the well-known arbiter of fashion in Savile Row. He was a remarkably agreeable and pleasant man, of superior manners, and most generous to all who knew him. He kept a good stud of weight-carrying hunters at Winslow, more for the pleasure of being ridden by his friends than himself, as he was not particularly noted in the pigskin. I have been told, and give it to my readers *cum grano salis*, that the late Emperor Napoleon owed his throne largely to the assistance of Count d'Orsay and Mr. Poole. It was said that the former was plotting and preparing the way for the advent of the prince in France, but that Mr. Poole weighed in with something like 10,000*l.* to provide ready money for his first requirements. At all events, whether this story be true or not, the prince succeeded in his object, and became a fast friend to Poole while he remained Emperor. Every month either Poole himself, or one of his representatives went over to Paris, and came back to England heavily laden with orders, and no man in Paris was at that time considered dressed unless he had a ' Poole ' coat on his back.

As an instance of the influence Mr. Poole exercised, I give the following story. The high sheriff of my county, the late Mr. Pennington, was over at Cherbourg at the time when the Emperor was entertaining her Majesty Queen Victoria, and a grand review of the French fleet was held, and a splendid ball was given on board the French admiral's ship, at which the Emperor, the Empress Eugénie, and our Queen were present. Everyone was most anxious to be among the distinguished party. The company was very select, and every effort was made to obtain a ticket of invitation. Poor Mr. Pennington was disconsolate at not being able to secure one, as he fully believed that as high sheriff for his county there would be no difficulty. He afterwards told me that, having exhausted every means he could think of, and having been always refused, some friend asked him if he knew Mr. Poole, saying that if anybody could get him an invitation he could. Poole happened to be Pennington's tailor, so he at once wrote to him, and he received by return the long sought for card of invitation, and a very kind letter from Poole, saying how gratified he was in being of service to an old friend. Mr. Pennington told me this story as an instance of the influence Poole had at the Emperor's Court. Poor Mr. Poole, after a most successful career in business, found out that the inordinate credit he had been almost forced to give had brought his finances to a very low ebb, and he sent to a friend of his, who was rich and a first-rate man of business, and laid the state of his affairs before him. He found that Poole was not only perfectly solvent but had a large and handsome surplus in his favour ; and he advanced him 20,000*l*., took the management of his finances in hand, and soon put the business on a firm basis, much to the delight of Mr. Harry Poole, who, however, did not live many years afterwards. Although high prices were charged for clothes, still I can testify, from many years of business connection, that when the heavy cash discount was taken off the charges were moderate, and the quality of everything superb.

In mentioning Count d'Orsay I am reminded of what Lord Beaconsfield says about him in 'Lothair':—

> He was one of the best friends he ever had, and not the least gifted. He was the most accomplished and the most engaging character that has figured in this century, who, with the form and the universal genius of an Alcibiades, combined a brilliant wit and a heart of quick affection, and who, placed in a public position, would have displayed a judgment and a commanding intelligence which would have ranked him amongst the leaders of mankind.

From what I personally remember of him in my youth, and the opinions I have heard expressed about him, I think the eulogy well deserved. He was one of the finest and handsomest men I ever saw, and when faultlessly dressed for the Royal Hunt Club dinner, in a scarlet dress coat, the skirts lined with white watered silk and faced with light-blue satin, a white waistcoat, and full black satin stock, high in the neck and throat, and black dress trousers, he was indeed inimitable. He once did me the honour to praise a chalk drawing of mine of a tiger in a cavern, copied from one of Stubbs's animal pictures, and promised that when he next came to Aylesbury he would bring me one of his own drawings. Before the next season the poor count had fallen from his high estate, and was obliged to leave England, his expenses having exceeded his income. He was remarkably fond of the Vale of Aylesbury, but he somewhat resembled his bosom friends the Lords Frederick and Adolphus FitzClarence, and their charming friend Poodle Wombwell, in not being amongst the first flight after the King's buckhounds. The meet, however, would not have been complete without the presence of such well-known men in the fashionable world, and their faultless costume, and the quality and character of the horses they rode, made a welcome addition to the brilliant assembly that was wont to gather together in the years 1835 to 1837, when his Majesty's and Mr. De Burgh's hounds visited that famous vale, now so ably and pleasantly hunted by Lord Rothschild.

Some years since, in the height of the poultry mania, I had some correspondence with her Grace the Duchess of Sutherland on the merits of the newly imported Bramah Pootras, as I was one of the first to bring this useful breed of poultry into prominent notice. Her grace wished me to give her my opinion on them, and as I had upon more than one occasion visited that gloriously beautiful seat, Cliveden, I determined to go and see my old friend Mr. Fleming, her grace's confidential manager and gardener of that lovely domain. In the end I presented her with a young cockerel and two pullets of the dark Bramah variety, and I believe they proved excellent denizens of the poultry-yard. One morning I received a letter from Mr. Fleming, saying that her grace had a handsome young 'Brahminee' heifer, which if I felt pleased to accept she would at once send to me. I felt much honoured by the offer, which I accepted, and one evening a few days afterwards I was astonished to see a large cattle van, drawn by two horses, standing at the door of my house in Aylesbury. I looked in and found a grand specimen of a large-sized Brahminee cow two years old. I had expected only to have had a little calf of one or two months old. I had the animal put amongst my herd of shorthorns, where she towered above them all, and with her beautiful countenance, large drooping ears, loose dewlap, and high hump on the shoulder, and her soft grey mouse-coloured skin, she became a prominent member of the herd. After a few days my shorthorns became accustomed to her, and during that summer she grew and flourished amongst them. I had intended and hoped to breed from her but was unsuccessful, and then decided to feed her and send her to the Islington cattle show at the following Christmas. This I did, and more attention was paid to this fine specimen of our Indian Empire than to the first-prize champion ox itself. She had become well fatted, and I sold her to a West End butcher for nearly 30*l.*, and a half of the *hump*, which with this breed of cattle is considered a great delicacy. The beef I heard was excellent. This, I believe, is one of the few attempts made to breed from the Brahmin tribe in this country. I found there were two breeds of this animal in India, the large and the small dwarf varieties, and this was one of the former. I heartily thanked her grace for her kindness, and Mr. Fleming for the trouble he had taken.

I may here state that the duchess and Mr. Fleming were two of the most eminent florists in England, and were the originators of our modern system of spring gardening. Mr. Fleming told me that the duchess had often complained that our flower borders were like fallow fields all the spring, and that everything was sacrificed to the bedding out of summer and autumn flowers; so the pair wandered forth in the umbrageous woods of Cliveden and selected the blue myosotis and the free-growing pink silene, and planted them in immense masses in the flower-garden. These they supplemented with the Cliveden white and yellow pansies, and by skilful combinations the fallow fields became gorgeous with these beautiful hardy flowers. I saw them once in early May, and I thought I had never seen anything so truly striking and of such soft and lovely colours as these wild plants of the woods. The great merit of the system is, that as soon as the flowers get shabby the plants are pulled up, the borders dug, and made ready for the geraniums, calceolarias, and other bedders for the remainder of the year. These, when removed in October, make way again for the spring flowers, and the gardens are beautiful all the year through.

In these days, when one of the most troublesome sanitary questions has to be solved, I am tempted to refer to my own experience on the question of sewage irrigation, or more properly the application or disposal of sewage refuse. I think I was one of the first who attempted to solve this very difficult question. Towards the close of the year 1852, his Royal Highness Prince Albert had taken up the question of sanitary improvement of towns, and had given his attention to the best means of purifying sewage. Mr. Yarrow, a civil engineer of some eminence, had suggested a plan of utilising the products by the filtration of sewage through peat charcoal. He had made arrangements with my neighbour the late Lady Frankland Russell, of Chequers Court, to carbonise a fine deposit of peat on her estates in Yorkshire, and he had brought the subject to the notice of the newly formed Board of Health in Aylesbury. That body agreed to try the experiment if anyone would find and pay for the charcoal. In my ardent enthusiasm I engaged to find it. The Board were to build proper filtering tanks, and I was to empty them at my own expense and have the manure for my trouble. It was found that one ton of peat charcoal would come out from the tanks as two tons, thus showing that the charcoal whilst the liquid sewage was passing through the tanks absorbed one ton of solid. A ton of peat charcoal properly granulated cost 3*l.* 10*s.*, and the expense of filling and emptying the tanks was about 10*s.* The two tons therefore cost 4*l.*, or about 2*l.* per ton. The first year I paid over 70*l.* for the charcoal, and I used the manure derived from it for every crop on the farm, and after my year had closed, *I found not the slightest value from its application.* The effluent water was clean and pure, the manure *odourless,* but *worthless.* I believe on analysis that the effluent was pure and tasteless, yet the water still held in solution the most valuable products, which all found their way into the stream and were therefore worthless. I have given the subject of the disposal of town sewage many years' study, and have visited most of the works in the large towns—the Craigentinny meadows at Edinburgh, the towns of Rochdale, Manchester, Wrexham, Banbury, Leamington, Bedford, Romford, and Croydon, and several others. I have studied all the chemical systems, by precipitation, filtration, &c., and am confident that *the only solution* of this most difficult and most important question is SEWAGE IRRIGATION. Where the sewage can be conducted and can fall by gravitation on the land, it will *be very profitable*, but directly you begin to pump and to lift it, then the expense begins, and the process takes away the greater part of the profit. I consider that, on the whole, the method in use at Croydon, Beddington, and Romford is the best I have seen at work, and I still think, if Colonel Hope's original scheme for carrying the sewage and refuse of our vast metropolis on to the Maplin Sands could be carried out at moderate cost, it would free the inhabitants of London from a serious trouble, and eventually could be made a profitable business. The earth-closet system in villages and country towns is an excellent process, but for London and the large towns the cost of carting ashes and earth for deodorisation would be enormous, and its removal practically impossible. After all, it is undoubtedly proved that water is the cheapest and most easy carrier of sewage, and it ought to be utilised wherever it can be done. Doubtless there is much trouble in getting land for sewage purposes, and an absurd idea is afloat that a sewage farm is *a nuisance*. Where the plan is properly carried out, it is quite devoid of deleterious influences.

I have discovered that the most useful and the most profitable crop for the disposal of sewage is that of osiers. These plants will drink up as much as you like to give them, and there is always a demand for osiers for every description of basket that enters into the uses of the people.

The strikes that have taken place continually in the coal districts, and the statements made as to the rights of labour, while at the same time ignoring the large amounts of capital sunk in developing the coal deposits in various parts of England, have reminded me of a story told to me by the late Mr. Joseph Robinson, at one time one of the leading proprietors of the Ebbw Vale Coal and Iron Company. It so happened that I was appointed one of the judges of cattle at the county show at Llanidloes, in 1876, and I well have cause to remember it, as it was the day after the election of a member for the county of Bucks in succession to the Right Hon. B. Disraeli, who had lately been created Earl of Beaconsfield, and had made on the day before his celebrated speech at our agricultural meeting, in answer to Mr. Gladstone's exaggerations of the Bulgarian atrocities. I was, I believe, the first voter to poll, when the poll opened at 8 A.M., that I might hurry off and catch my train for my South Wales duties. The poll was not declared till the next day, and I had arranged that a telegram should be forwarded to me in the show-ground as soon as it was declared ; and about four o'clock P.M. I received the announcement that the Hon. T. Fremantle, the Conservative candidate, had been returned by 187 over the Hon. Rupert Carington, the Gladstonian. I posted it up over the secretary's office, as during the day I was continually being asked as to the result, and I found it was on the whole very satisfactory to the assembled thousands. At the public dinner, after the show, in reply to the toast of the members of Parliament, a Mr. Davies rose to reply. He was a typical member of such a constituency as he represented, and I was much struck by his 'unadorned eloquence,' and his earnest, sensible, and straightforward speech. There were many, he said, in that room who knew him in a very different position from that which he now held, and, he was not ashamed to confess, there were many present for whom he had worked for a weekly wage, and he was proud to say in their presence he had never forgotten their kindness to him. He went on to speak of the pleasures of labour, and inculcated perseverance in adversity, and that men should not be cast down by circumstances that seemed insurmountable. His speech was loudly cheered, and I felt much interested in him, and on my return to a friend's house at Machynlleth, he told me that only a few years before Mr. Davies was a sawyer and carpenter. It happened that a bridge was required to be built over the river near that town, and as Davies was a clever fellow and a downright honest man it was suggested that he should tender for it. Davies objected that he had but slender means, but his friends had such confidence in his integrity that they found him the capital and he completed the work, and made a fair profit. Soon after the Cambrian railways were commenced, and he undertook a portion of the work, which he carried out thoroughly well. This encouraged him to undertake another section, and then another, until he had done the greater portion of the work and made a considerable sum of money. He then began on his own account to bore for coal in the neighbourhood of Swansea, and sunk his money rapidly, until he had spent all he had, and still no coal was found. Mr. Davies then determined to call his miners together and explain to them the cause of the abandonment of his venture. A large open-air meeting was held, and he addressed them in simple, plain terms, and told them he had spent the earnings of a life in the speculation.

A friend of mine, Mr. Robinson, said that he then held up between his thumb and finger *a half-crown*, and told them it was all that was left of 40,000*l.* which he had sunk in the mine, and that they had had it all, when a fellow brutally called out ' And we'll have that too.' ' So you shall,' he said, and pitched the half-crown up in the air, and thus threw it amongst them, and a great scramble took place for its possession. This bold action of his so pleased the men that they unanimously resolved to go on with the work at once, and fortunately in a few days they came upon a most valuable seam of coal, which soon recouped Mr. Davies for all his disappointment and great outlay. I have been told that no man was listened to in the House of Commons with greater attention than he was. I remember a portion of a speech he made on the discussion of a Bill for the abolition of ' the law of distraint.'

Although he was a thorough Liberal, he said he was not ashamed to own that if it had not been for the existing law of distraint he should not then have had the honour of addressing the House of Commons; that that law was oftentimes of the greatest value to a poor struggling man, especially a farmer; that in his early days he had got behindhand with the rent of his farm, but his landlord most kindly gave him more than two or three half-year's rent in hand, as he felt quite sure that he should lose nothing as the law gave him priority. This relief enabled him to turn himself round, and very soon he paid his arrears and became prosperous, and therefore he had every reason to speak favourably of the existing law. I can also corroborate Mr. Davies, as more than one instance has come under my knowledge, that when a landlord is kindly disposed it gives him the opportunity of helping a tenant when he has had, as is often the case, an unfortunately bad harvest.

Mr. Robinson who gave me the story of the 'halfcrown' was an excellent *raconteur*. He once told me a romantic story of a beautiful, virtuous, Irish girl, serving out whisky in a shebeen at the camp of Kildare. A sergeant fell in love with her, married her, was ordered to India at the outbreak of the Afghan War, and took her with him. He was killed at Jellalabad. The general saw the widow, became enamoured, and married her; he was created a baronet, she then became a Lady; he died. The widow gained the affections of a great peer, married him, and died. Thus the girl in the shebeen became a sergeant's wife, a baronet's widow, and ended her days as a marchioness.

CHAPTER VII

The Lowndes family—And Whaddon lawsuit—'The Writ of Right'—The reading of a tombstone—Serjeant Talfourd, afterwards a judge—Two dormant peerages—Whaddon Chase--Finding of Cymbeline British gold coins--The Kimbles—Great Roman Road—The Icknield Way, or Via Iceni—Bishop Wilberforce—An American's visit to the Chilterns—Visit to Ireland—An Irish agriculturist on the growth of beans—Rathkeale—'Greville Memoirs'—Account of Ireland.

I REMEMBER a great sensation was created in the county by a claim made against the Selby-Lowndes family for their property at Whaddon Chase, near Winslow. In or about the year 1770 old Adam Selby died, and left the estate to the Lowndes family, if the rightful heir could not be found. The law then in existence gave legal possession of a property which had for sixty years uninterruptedly held a good title. In the year 1830 a claim was set up by a pauper in Wales, a Mrs. Davies, and litigation commenced and lasted several years, sometimes the suit being decided in favour of Lowndes and sometimes of Davies. The claimant's case was from a Welsh pedigree, and went back for some centuries. At length it was tried by the ancient custom of 'The Writ of Right.' The jury were county gentlemen, and sat during the trial girt with swords and spurs. It was the last instance of this extraordinary custom being used. The celebrated counsel Serjeant Talfourd was for the

Lowndes family, and made a marvellously clever speech on this very remarkable and antique trial. The cause was settled in favour of the Selby-Lowndes family, and some time afterwards it was discovered that old Selby was illegitimate, and therefore had no rightful heirs, and the testamentary gift was perfectly legal and unimpeachable. I have been told of a remarkable circumstance that happened, which showed the shifts that were made to bolster up the case of the claimant. I believe that in tracing a pedigree, in the event of the parish registry failing, inscriptions on ancient tombs and tombstones are considered evidence, as also are insertions of births and deaths in well-authenticated family Bibles. A Welsh pedigree is notorious for its length, and often for its breadth, from the ramifications which are interlined. It happened that to fill one of the gaps in the Davies pedigree recourse was had to the inscription on a particular tombstone in a Welsh churchyard; a man was brought forward to prove that the dates of birth and death of a certain person were inscribed on it, that he had passed it every time he went to church, had read it, thus it had become thoroughly impressed on his memory. He very glibly gave his evidence, which appeared unimpeachable, when, if true, this link filled up and established a most important part of the claim. A happy thought struck Mr. Serjeant Talfourd, who had been reading 'The Times' newspaper in court, and he handed it up to the witness in the box, and, pointing to a certain paragraph, told the man to read it. The rascal looked at it, turned it round, then turned it upside down, and the learned counsel said, 'Go on, sir, read what I have given you,' and the man, completely beaten, gave the paper back. 'There, my lord, I thought so ; the fellow does not know how to read.' The judge indignantly ordered the witness to stand down, when, nothing abashed, he cried out, 'I can't read that printing, but only show it me on a tombstone, and I'll soon read it quick enough.' The plaintiff's counsel were completely taken aback by this false testimony, and I have heard it did more than anything else to damage the Davies case. It cost the estate a large sum to oppose the claim. The family prefixed the name of Selby to that of Lowndes, and it is now the distinguishing mark between the Whaddon and Chesham families. There are two dormant peerages in the family, viz. the baronies of ' Montague ' and 'Mount Thermor.' It is said that the litigation over this property gave the idea to Serjeant Warren for his delightful novel of ' Ten Thousand a Year.'

Some years ago the late William Selby-Lowndes inclosed a great part of Whaddon Chase, one of the few ancient forests remaining in England. When the land had been laid out in farms and was under tillage, a ploughman broke into an earthen pot with his plough, and scattered a large number of gold coins along the furrow. He picked some up, and put them in his pocket, and thought they were old buttons without shanks, and in the evening, whilst drinking a pint of ale in a public-house at Winslow, produced his tarnished buttons. A travelling clockmaker happened to be present, and gave the ploughman a pot of beer for one, and also sixpence each for all he had, and for as many more as he could

SIR JOHN EVANS AND THE WHADDON COINS 59

bring him. The man next day with his boy brought away a large quantity, and, the news having spread, others visited the field and a great many were secured, the price having risen to a shilling each. At last Mr. Lowndes heard of it and claimed it as 'treasure trove'; but he was too late, upwards of 800 had been sold and melted down. Yet in spite of this Mr. Lowndes managed to obtain over 400 for himself. They were found to be of the finest gold, and intrinsically worth fifteen shillings each, and proved to be of the reign of Kunobelin, or Cymbeline, immortalised by Shakespeare in the play of that name. Kunobelin, or Cunobelinus, the Latinised name of the Romans, was King of Britain at the time of the first invasion of this country by Julius Cæsar, 55 B.C. As I write these words I have in my scarf one of these identical coins fitted as a pin. It has a rude impression of a horse on one side, and on the other the usual wheat ear with other emblems. On some of the coins found was the word KUNO, showing unmistakably the authenticity of them. My friend Sir John Evans, the learned President of the Numismatic Society, pronounced them to be genuine, and selected a complete set of them, which were presented to the British Museum. The supposition is that they were the entire treasure of the king, which were probably intended for the payment of his troops, with general expenses, and were kept secretly by his treasurer; so when the king with his court and family were driven into the fastnesses of Whaddon Chase, the treasurer secreted them, possibly at the foot of some sacred Druidical oak, and was perhaps himself killed, and thus the money was lost; or possibly he might have forgotten the spot where he had deposited them, and there they lay for nearly two thousand years, until the ploughman brought to light these memorials of a great and stirring epoch in the history of our country.

I may remark, as an interesting fact, that about twenty miles from the spot where these coins were found are the two villages of Great and Little Kimble. These villages are at the foot of the Chiltern Hills, through which the great Roman road from Lactodorum (Stony Stratford), Dunstable, and Verulam (St. Albans) runs, thence by Wallingford (Watlingford) and Watlington to Devizes—a great Roman and British station—leaving the old town of Aylesbury (the Ægelsbireg of the Saxons) to the north on the direct road to Whaddon. Kimble, as its name implies, is 'Cymble,' or Kimbeline, and near it is a fine old British camp, where many remains of the Roman occupation of Britain have been found in the shape of coins, tessellated pavement, pottery, &c. I remember at the first meeting of the Bucks Archæological Society, under the presidency of the great Bishop of Oxford (Wilberforce), he said in a truly poetic strain, 'What so delightful as to travel over the spot where Arviragus marshalled his troops and Imogene twined her bower!' I once had four of these Cymbeline coins, and whilst showing an American gentleman the villages of Kimble, with the 'Icknield Way,' or 'Via Iceni,' passing through them, and the rich vale, as seen from the summit of the Chilterns, mapped out in fields by hedge-rows, and studded by farmsteads, villages, parish churches, thus forming an extensive landscape of great inland beauty, he exclaimed, 'Ah! now I see why you people love and are so proud of your country!' 'Yes,' I replied, 'that which you see has taken us upwards of fifteen hundred years to make, and we are naturally proud of it.' I then gave him one of my Whaddon coins, as a memorial that he stood on that spot over which the British king had often moved. A very perfect British camp is close by, which is still called 'Linus's Camp.'

Some years ago—it was in the year of the famine, 1847—I was employed in Ireland to serve notices for the Tilbury and Southend Railway. One notice I had to serve on a Mr. Burgess, a country gentleman living at Parkanaur, who knew my friends in Bucks, and who had been, singularly enough, educated at Beaconsfield. I was most hospitably entertained by him, and then returned to Dublin, and found I had to go almost to the extreme south. I went the first night to Kildare by rail, and thence in the morning by mail-coach to Limerick, the line only being opened to the former place; I was greatly interested in all I saw. I found in general agriculture much behind the age, but in some places fairly carried out. In the early morning I started after breakfast to walk on ahead, that the mail coach might overtake me, and had advanced about two miles on my road when I saw what I took to be a superior class of farmer lounging over a gate by the roadside, and entered into conversation with him, and learned that he farmed over 150 acres of land. The Government of the day were anxious to wean the Irish people from excessive growing of potatoes, and were desirous of teaching them to try other crops, especially field beans, and they had established depôts in different parts of the country, to supply the farmers and cottiers with seed beans at a low price, and I mentioned this fact to my agricultural acquaintance. He asked me the best plan to grow them, as he had heard a great deal about these beans, and intended to try them. I entered fully into the subject, giving him all the culture in detail, and showing him the great advantage of the crop as a complete change for the benefit of the land ; he listened with much interest, asked several pertinent questions, and said he was determined to try them. He then said, 'Sor, there is one thing I want you to notice: look round this part of the counthry, you see there's no trees about here.' 'No,' I said, 'nor any hedgerows.' 'Then what will I do for sticks?'

Here, then, was a well-to-do farmer, holding a hundred and fifty acres of land, who supposed the whole time I was explaining to him the mode of culture that I was telling him how to *grow kidney beans or scarlet runners*! No wonder the Government were anxious to improve the agricultural knowledge of the tillers of the soil. The coach took me up, after I had wished my farmer friend good-bye and begged him to try and grow beans for horses and pigs, and not for human beings. On arriving at Limerick I found I had to serve a notice on a soldier—I think of the 35th Regiment of Infantry ; he was not in the barracks, and the authorities thought he was at Ennis. On arriving there I discovered he was stationed at Rathkeale, and off I posted, going through a very picturesque country, especially around the town of

Adair. On arriving at Rathkeale, I found the right man, who was a corporal, drilling a squad of recruits. After explaining my business and treating him at a public-house, he signed the necessary documents; and giving him half-a-crown, with which he was highly delighted, I bade adieu to the towns of Rathkeale and Adair, and took up my quarters for the night at 'Cruise's Hotel,' at Limerick, and started by the mail in the morning for Dublin.

In the 'Greville Memoirs' occurs the following passage bearing on the position of Ireland in 1846 :—

> It is a record of a picture of manners and customs and fashions which are perpetually changing, and as establishing points of comparison and exhibiting contrasts and dissimilarities it may be curious and amusing. . . . . The state of Ireland is to the last degree deplorable and enough to induce despair. A people, with rare exceptions, besotted with obstinacy and indolence, reckless and savage ; all from high to low intent on doing as little and getting as much as they can ; unwilling to rouse and exert themselves ; looking to this country for succour, and snarling at the succour that they get. The masses brutal, deceitful, and idle ; while menaced with famine next year, they will not cultivate the ground, and it lies unsown and untilled. They were never so well off as this year of famine ; nobody will pay rent, savings-banks are overflowing ; with money they buy arms instead of food, *and then shoot the relieving officers.*

This is too sweeping a condemnation of the Irish people, and I only digress from my story of railways to show what was the feeling of so high an authority who held the distinguished office of Clerk to the Privy Council, and had better opportunities than most people of knowing the condition of the country.

CHAPTER VIII

Judges and the Bar—Lawsuit—London and North-Western Railway—Horace Lloyd—Staveley Hill—'The Straits of Malacca'—Lord Chief Justice Cockburn—and Mr. Serjeant Wells—Cock-fighting—The billeting of soldiers in an Assize town—Lord Chief Baron Pollock—The advent of judges to the assize towns past and present—Pedigree of Duke of Buckingham and Chandos—Charles Brandon, Duke of Suffolk—Marriage of Mary Tudor with Louis XII.—Public entry into Paris—Great rejoicing—Jousts and tournaments—Charles Brandon and English knights distinguish themselves—The Duke d'Alençon—Numbers of knights at the tournament—Charles Brandon unhorses the German giant—Death of the king—Marriage of Duke of Suffolk with the widowed queen—Return to England—Anecdote of great descent.

I WAS accustomed to ask the Bar to be my guests, after the White Hart was sold, and many a delightful evening my family had with them. On one occasion a very heavy law-suit was tried at quarter sessions, on the rating of the works at Wolverton of the London and North-Western Railway, and the late Horace Lloyd was specially retained for the parish, and Staveley Hill, who, I believe, is standing counsel for the company. The case lasted two days, and the two learned counsel, with the remainder of the sessions Bar, were my guests at dinner, and a most enjoyable evening it was. The brilliant wit and conversation of the party was long to be remembered; and we had a dance afterwards. It was about the time when a great deal of fun was made in Parliament with Disraeli's speech on the 'Straits of Malacca,' and Mr. Horace Lloyd sent me the following couplet, March 4, 1874 :—

> With *the* farmer of Aylesbury they sat down to dine
> On his excellent cheer and his capital wine;
> The mirth it ran high, and the fun was no slacker,
>   The laughter went round
>   With a loud cheering sound,
> And they ne'er gave a thought to the Straits of Malacca.

To which I sent the following doggerel reply :—

> Old Hodge drank his beer, and axed, with a sneer,
> 'Where be these here Straits of Malicker?
>   Dang Gladstone's sour wine!
>   Gi'e me malt and hop-bine,
> And don't tax a poor man on his licker.'

Poor Horace Lloyd's career, brilliant in the extreme, was cut short, and he died almost before middle age. Staveley Hill, I am glad to see, is still in the House of Commons, and dispenses the hospitality of Oxley Manor with true courtesy and kindness, as I can testify from personal experience.

My recollections of the Bar will not be complete without some reference to the judges when on circuit. On one occasion, when Lord Chief Justice Cockburn was at the assizes, he, in company with Mr. Serjeant Wells, had been walking with me over the farm. He came back to the White Hart to see my mare, a famous hunter of great beauty, and she excited his admiration. He was very fond of a good horse, and I have found many occupants of the Bench with a similar taste. I then told his lordship that the old inn had once an open gallery round the yard, and there were old people still living who remembered that the ladies of the town and neighbourhood were accustomed to fill the gallery, and look at the pastimes enacted on a stage in the centre of the yard, such as boxing, single-stick, and especially cock-fighting. Serjeant Wells said, 'There, my lord, you see our English ladies could look on at a cruel sport like that, whilst they blame the lookers-on at a bull-fight in Spain.' 'Gently, gently, Mr. Wells,' said the Chief; 'for my part I don't see the analogy, for I don't know better fun than to see a rattling good cock-fight between two combatants in a farmyard.' He chuckled heartily as he said this, and I told him I perfectly agreed with him.

On another occasion the assizes were being held, and the town was very full indeed, the White Hart, as usual, overflowing with guests, with every bedroom engaged. A message came that a regiment of cavalry was to march through the town, and the billeting sergeants came to the hotel and demanded accommodation for seven officers, eight men, and fifteen horses. I told them it was impossible to accommodate them, and they ought to go on to the next town, as I believed they had no right to stay in a town where the assizes were being held. They were exceedingly uncivil and rude, and said they had the right, and should take any bedrooms they pleased, as they had the first claim to them; and they took possession of the high sheriff's, which was the best in the house, for the colonel. I was very angry, and determined to appeal in person to the judges. I went into the judges' lodgings, which adjoined the house, and met the Lord Chief Baron Pollock and his brother judge just leaving the breakfast room in their full wigs and scarlet robes, going up the stairs to the court. Although greatly awed by their presence, I stated my case to his lordship, who listened attentively, and said he most certainly should not permit the high sheriff to be turned out of his room, as he was the representative of the sovereign, and had priority over everyone. He also said that I had his authority to stop any such proceedings, and that no juryman, nor anyone else actually engaged in the business of the assizes, was to be disturbed. The soldiers, he added, must think themselves fortunate if he did not order them out of the town. I was glad enough to hear this, and provided the officers with excellent lodgings at private houses at great personal loss, as we were paid nothing for our billets, and thus the affair ended; it is not generally known that the military have no right to be in an assize town during the assizes.

Since the introduction of railways the advent of the judges has been much shorn of its ancient pomp and ceremony. In my youth the high sheriff met the judges, about a mile out of the town, in a handsome coach, driven by a bewigged coachman, and four horses, the coachman and footmen in handsome liveries, and the sheriff's javelin men, also in livery, numbering about twenty-four. There was an old custom at Aylesbury, that a man, whose office was hereditary, carried a truss of wheaten straw, and placed it between the judges' carriage and that of the high sheriff, that he might step on it on leaving the one and entering the other The man was paid five shillings for this service, and it has been considered by some antiquaries to be the remains of the ancient charter of William the Conqueror to Aylesbury, that the town should furnish the king, should he pass that way, with three eels for his table, and *straw* for his chamber in the winter, and green rushes in the summer, and three green geese for his table.

My intimate relations with the late Duke of Buckingham and Chandos enabled me to ask him, somewhat familiarly, about his descent from the Plantagenet kings, and a short time after, and previous to his departure to assume the presidency of Madras, he called with his three daughters at my house to take luncheon with my family. I again broached the subject and he entered into further particulars, and I found it so interesting that I began to investigate it. I may say that I never knew a man who was so unostentatious in anything that appertained to his position, or who so little led you to suppose he was proud of his descent, as Richard Plantagenet Nugent Brydges Chandos Temple Grenville, Duke of Buckingham and Chandos. His grandfather was Marquis of Buckingham, and had married the only child of the last Duke of Chandos, the Lady Mary Brydges, and at the coronation of George IV. was created Duke of Buckingham and Chandos. The late duke was grandson of this first duke, and therefore lineally descended from the Chandos line, of whom one of the earliest, Sir Richard Chandos, was knighted on the field of Agincourt. The following details I have gleaned from various sources. A writer of the time of Henry VIII. says that the Princess Mary, sister of that monarch, and from whom the family of Chandos was descended, was beautiful, and that her beauty was the theme of universal admiration, and Henry had promised her to Charles, the grandson of Maximilian ; but the French King Louis XII. was anxious to wed her, and Henry thought it politic to accede to his wishes. Bacon relates in his history

that the Princess was doomed to experience the common fate of persons of her rank, whose passions and interests are often unrelentingly and unwarrantably sacrificed to state policy and the schemes of sordid ambition. After the affiancing by proxy she embarked for Calais, and Louis met her incognito at a short distance from Abbeville, and found that even the florid descriptions of her beauty fell short of the reality. He withdrew, and the Princess continued on her journey to the city, where she was met by the Duke of Valois on October 8, and her reception was greeted with processions and pageants becoming the occasion. Dressed in a gorgeous habit, mounted on a horse 'trapped in goldsmith's work very richly,' she made her entry, followed by thirty-six ladies of her retinue, of whom the ill-fated Anne Boleyn, then a child, was one. The archers of her guard, and the wagons loaded with her appointments, closed the train. On the following day, the festival of St. Denys, she was publicly married to Louis in the church at Abbeville. On the 5th of November following she was crowned in the Cathedral of St. Denys, and on the 6th she entered Paris as the Queen of France. The exertions which Louis made in his journey to receive the Queen brought on an attack of gout, and he was confined to his bed. Some alarming symptoms appeared, but his physicians were not much alarmed, although Louis himself realised that his end was near ; so he sent for the Duke of Valois, and embracing him tenderly, said : 'I am dying, I leave our subjects to your care,' and after a few hours of acute suffering expired in the arms of Francis, who never left his bedside.

Bacon continues :—

It was on the 1st of January, 1515, when she had been married only eighty-two days, that the youthful Queen was left a widow, and France lost one of her best kings.

While the public rejoicings for the accession of Francis I. were echoed throughout France, there was one heart which was unable to join in the general contentment. This heart belonged to the young dowager queen, not three months a bride, and yet a widow. She could not grieve deeply for Louis, and she saw that her free condition would expose her to new solicitations. The strength of her affection for Suffolk prompted her to a step full of peril. Without waiting for her brother Henry VIII.'s consent, and rather than endure the horror of another marriage in which her heart could not share, she offered her hand to Suffolk, who was still in France, and told him if he did not accept it in four days he never should have it. Suffolk hesitated, fearing to offend Henry, and Mary determined, if he refused, to enter a religious house. Suffolk, however, gave way, and at the risk of his head they were privately married. Mary wrote to her brother, told him how she had persuaded Suffolk, and took upon herself the whole blame. Henry pardoned them, and they were publicly married at Calais on their way back to England. So Mary returned, more happy in the possession of her love than she could ever have been even on the throne of France without it. It is from this marriage that the late Duke of Buckingham was descended in the Plantagenet line.

Our own chronicler, Hall, describes the entry of the young queen into Paris. I quote the extracts in the quaint spelling of the period, only somewhat modified. He says :—

It was Monday, the 6th day of November, that the said Queen was received into the city of Paris, after the order that followeth :

First, the guard of the city met her without St. Denys, all in coats of goldsmith's work, with ships gilt; and after them met her all the priests and religious, which were esteemed to be 3,000. The Queen was in a chaise, covered about (but not over her person) in white cloth of gold, the horses that drew it covered in cloth of gold, on her head a coronal of great pearls, her neck and breast full of jewels; then met her the Dauphin, the Duke d'Alençon, the Duke of Bourbon, Duke of Suffolk, Marquis of Dorset, Cardinals, and a great number of Estates, and so conveyed to the Cathedral, and went to her lodging for that night, and a great supper was provided; and after supper began dancing and pastime. On the morrow began the joustes, and the Dauphin entered the field with his aydes; the apparel and bardes were of cloth of gold, cloth of silver, and crimson velvet, cautled together in one suit. These joustes continued for three days, in which were answered 306 men of arms, and every man ran three courses—with sharp spears—and divers were slain, and none spoken of. The English lords and knights did as well as the best or any other. At the random or tourney the Duke of Suffolk hurt a gentleman that he was like to die; the Marquis stroke Mounsire Gun, an Albanoys, with his spear and pierced his headpiece, and put him in jeopardy; the Duke of Suffolk in the tourney overthrew a man of armes, horse and man, and so did the Lord Marquis another, and yet the Frenchmen would in no wise praise them. The Dauphin was hurt in the hand, and could not perform his challenge. The next day the Duke and Marquis began the field, and took the barriers with spears in hand, abiding all comers. The Dauphin brought a man secretly, which in all the court of France was the tallest and strongest man, and he was an Almayne (German), and put him in the place of another person, so to have the Duke of Suffolk rebuked. The same came to the bars fiercely with his face hid, because he would not be known, and bare his spere to the Duke with all his strength, and the Duke him received, and for all his strength put him by strong strokes from the barriers, and with the butt end of his spere strake the Almayne that he staggered, but for all that he strake strongly and hardly at the Duke, and the judges suffered many more strokes than were appointed, but when they saw the Almayne reel and stagger, then they let fall the rail between them.

The Lord Marquess of Dorset at the same time fought with a

gentleman of France, that he lost his spere, and in a manner withdrew; when the rail was let fall these two noblemen put up their visors for air; and then they took swords with points and edges abated, and came to the barriers, and the Almayne fought sore with the Duke, which imagined he was set on for the nonce; but the Duke by pure strength took him about the neck, and pommelled so about the head that the blood issued out of his nose, and then they were departed, and the Almayne was conveyed away by the Dauphin lest he should be known. These two noblemen of England fought valiantly divers feats, and the Frenchmen likewise nobly them defended; but it happened that the Lord Marquess one time to put for his aide his youngest brother, Lord Edward Grey, of the age of nineteen years, and to him was put a gentleman of France of great strength and stature, with intent to pluck him over the barriers, but yet the young lord was of such strength, power, and policy, that he so stroke his adversary that he disarmed at the face bare.

Hall in his Chronicles seems to revel in these scenes, and brings vividly before us the stirring events that happened in these tourneys. I cannot forbear quoting him in his description of the gorgeous apparel of the suites of many of the visitors. He says :—

Thus were these enterprises to the laud of all parties, and the Englishmen received much honour and no spot of rebuke, yet they were princely set on, and in many jeopardies; how goodly the coursers trotted, bounded, and quickly turned; how valiantly the men at armes behaved themselves, and how the Duke of Bourbon's bende was apparelled, and based in tawney velvet and cloth of silver cloudy; the bende of the Earl of St. Pol, apparelled and bended in purple velvet, all to cut on purple satten. The Dauphin and his aides were every day newly apparelled at his cost, one day in silver and gold, another in crimson and yellow velvet, and another in white velvet and green; some day mated in satin, some day embroidered, some day pounced with gold, and so every day in change as the workers' fancy could devise; but the English had ever on their apparel the red crosses, to be known for the love of their country; at this triomphe the County Galeas came into the place on a jennett trapped in blue satin, and he himself likewise apparelled, and ran a course with a spere, which was at the head 5 inches on every side square, that is 20 inches about ; and at the bar 9 inches square, that is 36 inches ; this spere was massy tymber, and yet for all that he ran clean with it a long course, and slightly annoyed it, to hys great honour.

Such was the account given by Master Hall in his chronicles of these splendid jousts and tournaments. How proud must have been the Princess Mary to see her newly-wedded husband carry himself so bravely ! I have somewhere read that the duke could unhorse any man in Europe except his king, Henry VIII. In the above description it appears that the duke, when he pommelled the Almayne, performed the feat described in pugilistic phrase of getting his head into Chancery.

The Lady Mary Brydges was married very early, and the marquis was also young, and I have heard in my youth that the parents with their first-born, the Marquis of Chandos, at a year old, altogether did not muster forty years of age between them.

Whilst speaking of the descent of great families I am reminded of a good story that was told of an unworthy descendant of the Duke de Montmorency, who was boasting that he was descended from the Constable de Montmorency, who was slain at Crécy, from a Montmorency who shed his blood at Agincourt, and from another who had fought under Turenne, when a bystander exclaimed, 'Is it not a pity how much you have descended ?' But this cannot be said of my friend the good Duke of Buckingham, who was the last of the race, and whose memory will be cherished by all who had the privilege of his friendship.

CHAPTER IX

Volunteers—My connection with the movement—Long service decoration as Quartermaster—Encampments—The Eton volunteers—Major Warre—Quartermaster Hale—The water drill—Gallant advance by swimming the Thames—Water polo—Capt. Durnford—Edwards-Moss—Remarkable trials—The Burnham murder—Moses Hatto—His death sentence—Curious circumstantial evidence—Jemmy Brookes, imprisonment for life—Duke of Buckingham's sword—Stealing a shroud—Sacrilegious robbery of lead from coffins—Jones, the Denham murderer—Coaching and Needle's murder—Horse-stealing—Soda and brandy.

ONE of the greatest movements of our time, and one which aroused the martial spirit of the nation, was the establishment of the volunteers. I can speak with some authority and confidence on this subject, as I joined the force at its commencement, and served for more than twenty-two years as a private and a sergeant, and for nineteen years held a commission as lieutenant and quartermaster, and was one of the first batch of officers receiving the long service decoration. I was with my regiment under canvas annually, and superintended their creature comforts during the encampment, which generally took place on the banks of the Thames, or some other of the rivers or waters in Bucks. Our colonels were able commanders and strict disciplinarians, and our camps were patterns of order and regularity. After the first few years of our annual muster the Eton College corps was encamped with the main body. These, with

Lieut. Hubbard, now Col. Lord Addington   Lieut. Horwood, now Lieut.-Col.   Col. Harrington, now Viscount Barrington   Qr.-Mast. Fowler retired   Ensign Wheeler deceased   Lieut. Marshal retired

GROUP OF OFFICERS, 1867

their officers, who were the masters of the college, numbered about eighty, and the major commandant was the Rev. J. Warre, now the head master, and my brother quartermaster was the genial Rev. E. Hale. I can safely assert that nothing more conduced to the perfect order and soldierly feeling in camp than the presence of the *Eton boys*, as we called them. They were models of soldierly discipline, and whether on guard at night, or as sentries over the water supply, or on ordinary camp duty, nothing could be more exemplary, and the young nobles and gentlemen of England were patterns of obedience to all with whom they came in contact. Not that the Bucks men were deficient in this respect; on the contrary, I maintain that no county could surpass them in discipline and obedience to orders, excellence at drill, and smartness on parade. I was assisted in my duties by a very excellent staff of quartermaster-sergeants, and our sergeant-major, Barkus, an old linesman, was indefatigable in doing everything necessary for perfection in camp life. As the Eton corps joined the officers' mess we sat down daily nearly 120, which made a goodly party. I cannot forbear mentioning some of the incidents of our annual outing, of which the most entertaining was the water drill of the Eton corps at seven in the morning. The line was formed on the banks of the river, their officers, as on parade, in the rear, all *in puris naturalibus*, and at the command ' The line will advance,' ' quick march,' ' charge,' the whole rushed forward and plunged into the Thames. Keeping their formation, the order ' fours right ' was soon given, and the company then ' formed line,' ' out the markers,' ' by your right,' and this continued, and was carried on in the water in the most perfect manner, till the order 'The line will retire,' 'dismiss,' when fun and frolic ensued, floating and swimming as only *ducks* and *Etonians* can, until they rushed on land, dressed, and ate such a breakfast as would gladden the heart of man to see. The water polo in the evening was performed in canoes, and in bathing costume, and the greatest frolic was towards the end of the game, when there was a general *mêlée*, and the chief aim was to upset Captain Durnford's canoe, and to give that worthy and cheery master a ducking.

On one occasion these aquatic performances culminated in a feat which had been considered impossible with the rifle by infantry soldiers. Early one morning it was arranged that about fifty of this corps should cross the river at Medmenham, and defend a supposed fort from attack, and a detachment was to advance and dislodge them. The former were ferried over in large punts, whilst the attacking party proceeded up the river, perfectly nude, except that they had their cartouche boxes on and rifles in hand. Stealthily they crept along the bank, and quietly entered the river, supporting their rifles against their chests with the left hand, and noiselessly with their right hands swam across the Thames, crept among the rushes which lined the banks of the stream, and like white Kaffirs stole ashore, and lying down fired at their opponents, to the dismay and astonishment of the garrison. A second volley was poured into them and a rushing charge was made across the open, accompanied by loud shouts, and the camp was carried by assault, the defenders little thinking of this daring manœuvre, nor that it was possible to fire a rifle after being immersed in the river, and with cartridges which had been completely wetted. It was thus practically proved that the breechloader, although wetted, could be almost as dangerous as before. I must not omit to mention one daring act performed by Edwards-Moss, afterwards famous in the rowing world, who, *in full uniform*, shako on head and sword in hand, sprang into the river, and with his left hand swam across and gallantly led his men to the charge. On the return of the captured garrison it was amusing to see the victors, as they brought their prisoners across the river, swimming and gyrating round the punts like so many Tritons and other emissaries of Neptune. Since this time the Eton corps has become the 2nd Bucks, and the genial and athletic commander, Major Warre, is now head master of the college, resigning his sword for another emblem more befitting his new duties, but now little used, to the dismay of the shade of ' Keate ' of birching fame. In concluding, I can safely assert that the meetings in camp were amongst the most delightful of my reminiscences ; my brother officers were agreeable companions and indefatigable in their duties, and the three colonels, Barrington, Chester,[1] and Wethered, were commanders worthy of all praise. Three of the officers are now peers of the realm, Viscount Barrington and Lords Cottesloe and Addington, and I am convinced that in my day nothing has tended more to raise the physical and moral position of the youth of England than the establishment of the volunteers.

[1] Now no more.

As an instance, amongst many others, of the strict discipline practised by the Bucks Volunteers, especially with the Eton boys, when in camp, it happened that the volunteers of the counties of Northampton and Bucks united one year and encamped in the Duke of Buckingham's park at Stowe. The late Duke of Grafton was colonel of the North Hants regiment, and Wethered was colonel of the Bucks. On one side the camp was divided by a 'haw-haw,' or sunken fence, from the ornamental grounds of Stowe, and a few planks were laid across to form a temporary bridge for the officers to pass to the mansion. Strict orders had been issued that no one was to cross the bridge without a pass signed by the commanding officer. It so happened that on a certain evening the quarter-guard for this bridge was furnished by the Eton corps, and the non-commissioned officer in command saw a tall gentleman in plain clothes coming towards the temporary bridge, and on attempting to cross it he was stopped by the sentries on duty. The intending passenger said, 'I am the Duke of Grafton.' 'We don't care for that; you are not in uniform and we have no proof of it; where's your pass?' The duke said, 'I am Colonel Commandant of the camp, and must pass.' The guard was turned out and formed on the bridge and bayonets were fixed, and his grace found it impossible to proceed, and good-humouredly told them, 'He would get a pass from the adjutant'; which he did, and the duke complimented them afterwards for their strict adherence to orders, as it was only the second day they had been in camp, and he was quite unknown to them. I have often remarked that on all occasions these scions of our aristocracy set an example of obedience that was not lost on their comrades.

Living as I did in a county town, and my residence in my childhood adjoining the county prison and courts of justice, I had many opportunities of hearing remarkable trials, and at the risk of being accused of relating gruesome stories I cannot refrain from mentioning one or two, which contain some singular circumstances. Some years ago a Mr. Ralph Goodwin, who was a schoolfellow of mine, and was a first-class gentleman farmer, and a bachelor, residing at Burnham, near Maidenhead, went out one night on horseback to dine with a friend. He left his worthy housekeeper at home with his young groom, Moses Hatto, and on returning home, about twelve o'clock at night, he gave his horse to the groom. On entering his house he discovered a strong smell of something burning, and on going upstairs found his housekeeper dead on the hearth, her knees and the lower part of her body much burnt, and her clothes and some of the furniture in flames. After putting out the fire he called his man, who at first did not obey the summons. He then discovered dreadful wounds on the poor woman's head and throat; her hands also were frightfully cut, as though she had defended herself, and many marks of blood were found on the staircase, showing she had struggled to get upstairs. Hatto said somebody must have broken into the house to rob it, and had murdered her. Mr. Goodwin sent him off for the police, and they at once suspected the real criminal. Hatto was despatched to Maidenhead for the doctor, and on his return was taken into custody, searched, and examined specially to see if there were any marks of blood on his clothes; but nothing could be discovered, except that the bottom of the legs of his trousers were wet and dirty, which he explained had been caused by passing through the farm-yard. There were many circumstances that told very strongly against the prisoner. The fact of his having paid his addresses to the housekeeper, who had more than once refused him, of his having been heard to threaten her life, and the fact that he was sitting up alone with her, waiting for his master, were very damaging, while there was no evidence whatever that anyone else had been seen on or about the premises. Serjeant Parry defended Hatto, making an eloquent appeal to the jury, and dwelling most forcibly on finding no marks of blood on any part of his clothing, and almost hinting that it was quite possible that the master himself had done the deed. The judge summed up very carefully, and protested against the bare suspicion of the crime having been perpetrated by Mr. Goodwin; the jury found the prisoner 'guilty,' and he was duly sentenced to death. From the dock in which the prisoners are tried is a trap-door and ladder leading down into the prison. Mr. Sherriff, the governor, went down with the prisoner, who, as soon as they arrived at the bottom said to him, 'Oh! sir, I am guilty. I was so shocked at my counsel calling the attention of the jury to my having no blood on my clothes that I was almost bursting to cry out, "Don't believe him, gentlemen; I did do it, I did do it." Now, sir, look here.' He then showed his underclothing, which he had concealed from the police, and even from the prison authorities, and his drawers were covered with blood. 'Now, if the police will search under the manger of the stable they will find the stones have been removed, and my shoes are there, as also my waistcoat, and under the culvert of the nearest gateway to the house they will find my stockings, and when I went over Maidenhead Bridge I dropped my shirt, with a big stone in it, into the Thames; that is how I got rid of my clothes.'

Mr. Sherriff told the police, who professed to have diligently searched the premises, and on examining the places indicated everything was found exactly as the prisoner had described; all were saturated with blood. So much for the examination of the police! Before his execution Moses Hatto was deeply penitent, and said he committed the murder in a fit of passion at his victim's refusal to marry him, and saying she loved some one else better than himself. Poor Mr. Goodwin's mind was so unhinged at the bare suspicion of his being guilty of the crime that he lost his reason, and ended his days in an asylum. So concluded this terrible tragedy. I have written this account to show on what slender threads conviction sometimes rests, and how culpably careless the police and prison officers sometimes were in examining the clothing of prisoners.

I remember in my boyhood seeing in the county gaol a man named Brookes, who was tried for shooting at a man in his father's employ; he was acquitted on the ground of insanity, and ordered to be imprisoned for life. He was incarcerated for more than twenty years, and never saw a green field or a living creature, except those inhabitants, both human and otherwise, who dwell in prisons; and when the new prison was erected and the old one destroyed, he was pardoned. I remember seeing him when he was discharged, a good-looking specimen of a hearty countryman; he appeared dazed, and scarcely knew what to do with himself. His friends came to meet him and took him home to the farmhouse where he was born. Until this unfortunate fracas took place, Brookes had borne a good character. He lived little more than a year after his liberation, and would probably have existed many years longer had he continued in his old methodical habits whilst in gaol.

I have touched but lightly on some sensational trials of prisoners, but cannot refrain from mentioning others that I venture to think were quite unique in their character. When the father of the late Duke of Buckingham—who was the second duke—died, his yeomanry sword, which was a very handsome and valuable one, presented to him by his brother officers and the men of the Bucks Yeomanry, of which he was the beloved colonel, was buried with him. The sword, being laid on his coffin, was placed in the vault in Wotton Church and built up in the usual way. Some time after the funeral it was observed that the masonry of the vault had evidently been tampered with, and on investigation it was found that the sword was gone! A great stir was at once made about it, but no trace could be found. Suspicion fell on no one, and every inquiry was prosecuted by the police all over London and elsewhere; still, nothing could be heard of the valuable weapon. At last, from some hints having been dropped by a farm labourer in the parish over his beer in a public-house, the man was taken into custody, whereupon he confessed that he had broken into the church, made his way to the vault, and abstracted the sword, and when he had secured the prize he dared not offer it for sale and had for very fear hidden it in the thatch of a barn or outhouse, where on examination the sword was found intact. The man was sentenced to a short term of imprisonment and the precious object was returned to its resting-place.

Another gruesome felony was perpetrated at Buckingham, namely, the stealing of a shroud from a dead body. As far as I can recollect, the facts of the case are as follows :—An old maiden lady had died possessed of considerable property, and there was a clause in her will to the effect that previous to her burial she was to be wrapped in a fine woollen shroud, and then a white satin ditto embroidered with Buckinghamshire lace. Her wishes were scrupulously attended to, and the body so clothed was placed in the coffin. Before it was screwed down, the family came to take a last look at their late relative, and having stayed some time they left the room. It was stated by the undertakers' workmen that their master remained after the family had left, and then removed the two shrouds from the body. On examining the coffin the next day, before the funeral, the shrouds were missing, and the undertaker was tried for the crime. The celebrated Serjeant Wilkins was specially engaged for the defence, and suggested to the jury that it was the men who had done the deed, and had tried to fix it on their master, who bore an irreproachable character in the town. The result of the trial was that the undertaker was acquitted and his men found guilty.

Perhaps a more gruesome crime was the following, committed not more than six or eight years ago. The church of Brayfield, near Newport Pagnell, was under restoration, and certain alterations were necessary in the chancel, and the tomb of the Farrers, the old county family residents of the parish, was to be partially removed. After the foreman had left, the workmen removed the coffin of the late squire into the chancel, together with the coffins of two other members of the Farrers family, broke them open, and took out the bodies. They then carried off the leaden shells of the coffins, which were valuable, and left the bodies lying about in the chancel, where they were seen next day by their foreman. Suspicion fell on some of the workmen, but they all stoutly denied the charge. It was, however, known that some of them had offered some old lead for sale, and so they stood for their trial at Aylesbury assizes. A curious point as to the ownership of the lead was raised by counsel on behalf of these rascals, viz. to whom did the lead belong? It could not belong to the dead squire, and the young squire had parted with his property and deposited it in the church. The judge, however, held that the indictment was good, and, if not, they could have been indicted for sacrilege, which would have entailed even a heavier punishment than that he was about to inflict, and I believe they were sentenced to long terms of imprisonment with hard labour.

Some few years ago all England was shocked at

the perpetration of perhaps one of the most dreadful murders ever heard of in the annals of brutal crime. This awful tragedy was called the 'Denham Murder.' Here is a brief outline of the facts from memory. Denham is a very picturesque village near Uxbridge, from which it is separated by the river Colne. In this place resided the village blacksmith, Marshall by name, with his smithy adjoining his cottage. With him resided his wife, the grandmother, and four children. On a certain Sunday it was observed by the neighbours that the family, contrary to their usual custom, were absent from church, and as no one had been seen in or around the house, suspicion arose that something wrong had happened. The door of the cottage being forced open, a dreadful sight presented itself. At the foot of the stairs and in the sitting-room lay the bodies of Mrs. Marshall, the old grandmother, and four children. The place was like a slaughter-house; all were found with their skulls fractured and so frightfully battered about the head and face as to be almost unrecognisable. The father was missing. Suspicion, of course, at once fell upon him, and it was at once concluded that this direful crime could only have been perpetrated by him in a fit of insanity, inasmuch as he lived on the most affectionate terms with his wife and family, and was of an exemplary industrious character. A search was made for him everywhere; and at last, on looking into the blacksmith's shop, his body was found quite dead and his head much battered about. The doors of both the house and the shop were found locked and the keys missing, so Marshall's pockets were searched, but no keys were found, and from the frightful injuries on his head it was certain that they could not have been self-inflicted. It did not appear that any money had been stolen, and it seemed quite a mystery, until it was stated that a journeyman smith, who had formerly worked for Marshall, had been seen near the house the evening before. This man was a notoriously bad character, and had been discharged for his drunkenness and idle habits. He was traced to Uxbridge to a lodging-house, where he had slept on the Saturday night and had left during the Sunday; from thence he was traced to Reading, where he had been seen in company with a woman of bad character, and was taken into custody by the police, and on searching him the keys of the house were found upon him, and some trifling things which he had brought away with him from the scene of his wholesale slaughter. He was committed for trial at the summer assizes at Aylesbury, and was found guilty. From the facts which came out at the trial, and from remarks which he made after his condemnation, it appeared that John Jones had applied to Marshall for work. This had been refused on the ground of his bad reputation. He then from revenge struck the blacksmith with a hammer, rendering him senseless, and then battered his head with a sledge-hammer and left the body in the workshop. He then went into the house and beat the poor wife to death. The children, who had gone to bed, hearing something unusual, came downstairs, and the murderer, standing at the foot of the stairs, struck them with the hammer one by one as they came down-stairs. Finally the poor old grandmother, hearing a noise, came down from her room, and met with the same fate. I have been told, by one who was present at the execution, that there were four or five steps leading up to the scaffold, that the murderer ran up these, and, placing himself under the beam, stood quietly, till Calcraft, the executioner, adjusted the rope round his neck, and when the cap was pulled over his face he said, ' I wish to say something.' The cap was lifted up from his mouth, and he said, ' I didn't murder 'em.' The drop was drawn and in a few seconds this monster ceased to exist, dying with a wilful lie on his lips, and thus ends the story of one of the most diabolical murders ever recorded in our county. I should have mentioned, in addition to other strong evidence, that the damning fact came out, that at the time of his capture he was wearing poor Marshall's boots, which he had taken off his victim's feet after the murder. This evidence alone would have been enough to hang the wretch.

One morning in January 1824, Wyatt's coach, the old Aylesbury ' Despatch,' left the town as usual about seven o'clock, the morning being cold and wintry ; and after proceeding about one and a half mile arrived at the first turnpike gate, kept by a worthy old fellow named Needle. Although but a mere child at the time, I remember the circumstance well. The old gatekeeper, whose custom it was to stand at the door with the turnpike gate thrown open to let the coach through, on this morning was absent. Mr. Wyatt, the coachman, got off the box seat, and, after knocking repeatedly and getting no reply, burst open the door, when a shocking sight met his view : the body of the old man was lying on the floor, his head dreadfully beaten about, and he was quite dead. The coachman on entering the bedroom saw the body of Needle's wife lying across the bed, her head cruelly crushed, and quite bereft of life. Very near the turnpike was Broughton Farm, a farm my family occupied some years after these events. Wyatt at once gave the alarm, and the farm men hastened to the spot; the coach in the meantime kept on its way to London, carrying the information to every place on the line of road. It was quickly reported that two suspicious gipsy-looking people had been seen going towards the toll-bar late on the previous night, and the same men had been seen at daylight returning through the town of Tring. They were overtaken near Hemel Hempstead, and a silver watch and about four shillings in money was found upon them. The watch was identified as having belonged to the old people, and as blood was found upon their clothes but little doubt remained that they were the murderers. A few weeks afterwards their trial took place at Aylesbury, and they were found guilty and executed. It appeared, by their confession before their execution, that they had calculated that the takings of the week at the turnpike, which would have amounted to three or four pounds, would have been found there, but Needle had only the day before carried the money to the lessee of the tolls, so the poor old people's lives were sacrificed for a few shillings. They managed to get into the house by leading a horse with a halter on him, which horse they had caught in a field at Broughton Farm, and arousing the inmates by calling to them to open the gate. The old man in his nightshirt came and opened the door, when they knocked him down with the head of a hurdle, which they took from a cowhouse at the farm. This they roughly formed into a bludgeon, and with it they did their bloody work.

Coachmen in those days were oftentimes the means of the detection of crime, as they carried news of any serious offence to every village and roadside inn along which they passed, and this was especially so in cases of horse-stealing, as the coachman or guard often noticed the horses going along the road, and, provided they had news of the robbery, they often were able to give information which led to its detection. I remember one very noted case of two horses being stolen at Lutterworth in Leicestershire, which were seen by the coachman of the old Leamington and Warwick coach, who even took a man who was with them into the town of Aylesbury. This man was tried at the assizes, found guilty, and transported for life. In connection with this case a most extraordinary thing happened. The prosecutor was a county gentleman who occasionally indulged in an outbreak of excessive drinking; he came up from Lutterworth with his medical man, who was himself owner of one of the stolen horses. This county squire during the assizes stayed at the White Hart, and during the day, from 6 A M. to 11 P.M., consumed fifty-seven glasses of soda-water and brandy. I have the bill now by me and can vouch for the fact.

CHAPTER X

Gastronomy—Mr. John Kaye—High Sheriff—His dinner—The Trafalgar at Greenwich—Emperor sherry—Whitebait—Mr. Hart—Baron Meyer de Rothschild—James McConnell—Floral decorations—Railway banquet—Mr. H. W. Lawson's coming of age—Late Henry Brassey—Lord Mayor's banquet at the Mansion House—Luncheon at the Kalenberg, Vienna—And bills of fare.

IT has often struck me that there are other men besides kings, orators, statesmen, warriors, and great lawyers, who have had their share in altering old ideas and forming new ones, unostentatiously but surely, and I would mention as an instance Mr. John Kaye, whom it was my good fortune to know intimately when I was a young man. When Mr. Kaye was high sheriff of Bucks, in the year 1853, he was anxious to give a banquet such as had never before been seen in the county; in fact, he wished to bring 'the city' down into 'the country.' Mr. Kaye had retired from business with an ample fortune, and took up his residence at 'Fernacres,' near Gerrard's Cross, and he arranged that this dinner should take place at the White Hart, and that Mr. Hart, of the Trafalgar at Greenwich, with his staff of cooks and assistants, should come down to Aylesbury for the occasion and show the nobility and magistracy of the county what a modern repast should be like. Mr. Kaye had formerly been the proprietor of the Castle and Falcon, in Aldersgate Street, and in the early part of the present century built the Albion Tavern, nearly opposite, with its magnificently furnished rooms, and established a cuisine and stock of wines that were matchless. On building the Albion he was determined there should be such an establishment for high-class dinners as should surpass any of the then existing clubs, or the tables of the highest in the land, and he succeeded in his purpose. The Prince Regent often honoured the establishment with his presence, and I believe it was the only place of public entertainment he ever entered.

A propos of the Prince Regent and the Albion I have heard Mr. Kaye tell an interesting story. During the great war, about 1810, a French merchant-ship was taken prisoner by a British privateer as she was sailing from Cadiz and bound for Havre, and amongst her miscellaneous cargo there were on board of her two butts of remarkably fine brown sherry of the highest quality, which had been specially shipped for the use of the Emperor Napoleon. These were given to the Prince Regent, who had one butt bottled for his own cellars, and the other was sent to the Albion to be bottled for his use, and that of his special friends, when dining there. Several dozens of this superb wine had been left at the Albion, and the high sheriff thought it an excellent opportunity to regale his friends with it at this assize dinner, and delicious it indeed was after about forty years in bottle. At the termination of his shrievalty about eighteen bottles were left, which he presented to my father, and I have two bottles of it in my cellars now. This wine is nearly one hundred years old, and I must say it has never been my lot to drink anything finer than this glorious brown sherry, and the modern style light dry wines are poor indeed in comparison with the generous wealth of flavour and character that this wine shows. On the occasion above mentioned Mr. Kaye gave his guests a real Greenwich dinner, including whitebait, a dainty unheard of before, I believe, in the county of Bucks, and generally no expense was spared, special messengers bringing down the fish and the ice from London. Mr. Hart, who kept the Trafalgar at Greenwich for many years, was placed there by Mr. Kaye, whose brother was an architect, and had designed it. The Trafalgar was the noted house for the ministerial whitebait dinners for a long series of years, but changes of fashion and custom have caused it to be closed, and those who have had the opportunity of dining there can testify to the high quality of the viands and the superiority of the wines which characterised the management.

Shortly after the shrievalty of Mr. Kaye, the Baron Meyer de Rothschild was appointed high sheriff of Bucks, and he gave a series of very *recherché* dinners at the White Hart, both at the winter and summer assizes. The dinners were chiefly remarkable on account of their having been dressed by his French *chef*, M. Chardonnel, of Parisian fame. I have not the bill of fare, but have in my possession his little bill *for extras* for two of the dinners. This small account came to 37*l.* 15*s.*, and the items would give the learned in such matters some idea of the provisions for the occasion. This succession of banquets did not end here, and the lavish display was kept up by succeeding high sheriffs, who, as county gentlemen, did not like being outdone by the Hebrews, nor by the *nouveaux riches*, who had lately come to reside in the county.

The dinner given by 'Squire' Drake to about seventy gentlemen was memorable as being the last banquet of the then prevalent style of dining, there being twenty-six dishes of fish as one of the courses. After this Mr. Tyringham gave a dinner in the new style *à la Russe*, and it was prepared by Messrs. Gunter. The table was adorned with handsome plate and centre-pieces, and richly decorated with flowers and fruit, and was a novelty to the country gentry; but it was speedily adopted by them, and became prevalent not only in Bucks but in the adjoining counties. I append a menu of Mr. James McConnell's dinner, which he gave in the Corn Exchange at Aylesbury when he served as high sheriff.

POTAGES
Tortue et Tortue claire

POISSONS
Anguilles en Matelote   Truite à la verte
Saumon de Gloster bouilli   Turbot, Sauce de Homard
Eperlans frits

ENTRÉES
Vol-au-vent de Ris de Veau et Truffes
Epigrammes de Cailles à la Périgueux

RELEVÉS
Poularde à la Régence
Petits Poulets rôtis   Jambon sauté au Vin
Hanches de Venaison

RÔTS
Dindonneau piqué   Oisons   Canetons

ENTREMETS

Crevettes en buisson   Suédoise aux Fruits
Pâtisserie à la Vénitienne
Meringues à la Crème
Gelée au Marasquin
Croûtes aux Fraises

RELEVÉS

Pouding à la Nesselrode
Anchois

It has been my good fortune, from my connection with short-horn cattle-breeding, to become associated with some of the leaders of that fascinating and patriotic pursuit. I have shown in other portions of these reminiscences how remarkably short-horn cattle had become a fashion, and how frequent were the sales of the leading breeders. At these sales excellent and substantial luncheons were provided, oftentimes of a *recherché* description, and as my reminiscences are a record of the times in which I lived, it may not be out of place to insert a chapter chiefly on gastronomy ; and, on a perusal of the menus which are appended, it may tend to show how the world lived and moved in the 'fifties' and onwards. I feel sure that in no portion of the household have greater improvements been made than in the dining and provisioning of the guests of a gentleman's mansion. I have elsewhere given an account of the origin of the 'Bates' short-horn dinners, and append a menu, at which I had the honour of dining with twenty-three others. Amongst those who dined, and were all distinguished breeders of short-horn cattle, were the Duke of Devonshire, the Marquis of Exeter, Lords Lathom,

Dunmore, Bective, Penrhyn, Feversham, and Braybrooke, Mr. T. Brassey, M.P., Col. Kingscote, M.P., Messrs. Angerstein, M.P., E. Bowley, &c., &c. The 'Bates' dinners were continued for several years, but are now shorn of all their glory ; many of those who led the van in this pursuit are gone to their long home, and the depression in the condition of agriculture seems to have taken the 'go' out of all those connected with the cultivation of the land.

     A la Tortue claire et liée
       A la Julienne
   Le Saumon, Sauce purée de Homard
     Les Blanchailles frites

  Les Côtelettes de Volaille à la Clarendon
  Les Ris de Veau piqués à la Financière

   Les Selles de Mouton de Clun
      Le Bœuf rôti
   Les Poulards à la Maltaise
   Le Jambon au Vin de Madère

      Les Asperges
    Les Salades de Homard
    Les Œufs de Pluvier

    Les Beignets d'Abricot
    Le Vol-au-vent de Gelée

    Les Biscuits glacés
   Les Ramequins de Parmesan

      Les Harengs
      Les Merluches

This dinner was given at the Clarendon by the Earl of Lathom.

When the Bill for leave to build the London and Aylesbury line was passed through Parliament, a great dinner was held to celebrate the occasion at the Trafalgar, and the late Duke of Buckingham and Chandos was in the chair, and Sir Edward Watkin in the vice-chair.

WINES	
Punch	
Madeira	
Amontillado	
HOCK :	
Marcobrunner	
CHAMPAGNE :	
Pommery	
and Giesler's	
Liqueurs	
PORT :	
vintage 1840	
CLARET :	
vintage 1864	
Gold Sherry	

POTAGES
Tortue claire   Tortue liée
Gras vert au Jus
POISSONS
SOUCHETS
Truite   Carrelets
FRITURES
Rissolettes de Homard   Anguilles à la Diable
Petites Soles
ENTRÉES
Matelote d'Anguilles à la Bordelaise
Boudins de Merlans décorés
Côtelettes de Saumon à la Trafalgar
Truite à la Beyrout   Turbot à la Vatel
RELEVÉS DE POISSONS
Omelette à la Blue Seal
Saumon à la Norvégienne   Les Ablettes
ENTRÉES
Bouchées de Ris de Veau à la Bohémienne

SECOND SERVICE
Selle de Mouton
Jambon braisé au Vin de Champagne
Poulets de Printemps   Canetons
Beans and Bacon
ENTREMETS SUCRÉS
Gâteaux fondants   Meringues à la Chantilly
Gelées au Marasquin
Pouding glacé à la Macédoine
GLACES
Pain Brun glacé   Crème de Framboises
L'Eau d'Orange
DESSERT
Grapes, Peaches, Strawberries, Cherries,
Apricots, &c.

As usual in a Greenwich dinner, fish was an important element, and it will be observed that the wine accompanying each course is in the margin.

Here, too, is a luncheon at a short-horn sale at Underley Hall, Westmoreland, the private residence of the late Earl of Bective. This was served cold, and was partaken of by upwards of five hundred guests in a large tent.

Rounds of Beef
Hams with Aspic
Roast Beef
Tongues with Aspic
Terrines of Hare
Terrines of Partridge
Game Pies with Jelly
Raised Veal and Ham Pies
Nerac Pies with Jelly
Roast Lamb and Mint Sauce
Mutton Pies
Roast Geese
Roast Ducks
Roast Partridges
Pickled Salmon
Salmon, Sauce Tartare
Lobsters, Sauce Mayonnaise
Babas with Rum
Greengage Tarts
Pastry
Plum Cakes
Potatoes
Green Salads

I can also testify to the perfect taste and elegance of the dinner-table decorations in the house, where a party of about forty-five assembled for two or three days. The earl's charming countess superintended and designed the decorations of the table, which consisted on the first day of corn and corn-flowers; the second day, of grape vines laden with fruit in pots, the table being under a bower of growing vines; the effect of this was superb. The decorations on the third day were very novel and singular, pots of beautifully grown capsicums trained about a foot and a half high, and covered with bright yellow fruit hanging down from a canopy of the most shining green foliage. These on a scarlet cloth had a charming effect. The dessert was laid on strawberry leaves, melons and grapes being placed on the centre scarlet cloth, and so the necessity was avoided of placing dishes among the handsome plate, candelabra, and silver centre-pieces. The room was lighted by more than three hundred wax lights in chandeliers and silver sconces round the room.

On the coming of age of Mr. Harry Webster Lawson, M.P., at the seat of his father, at Hall Barn, near Beaconsfield, a large party of the tenantry, the gentry of the neighbourhood, and his personal friends in the county assembled by invitation to an elegant and substantial dinner on December 18, 1883.

   Julienne Soup   Mock Turtle Soup
    Salmon à la Parisienne
    Lobster Mayonnaises
   Fillets of Soles à la Princesse
    Prize Baron of Beef
   Turkeys farcis aux Truffes
  Roast Fowls   Roast Ducks
  Roast Pheasants   Roast Geese
    Boar's Head

York Hams   Ox Tongues
Braised Beef   Game Pies
Fillets of Veal à l'Anglaise
Galantines of Fowl
Rabbit Patties à l'Américaine
Galantines of Veal
Salads   Vegetables

Plum Puddings   Mince Pies
Babas au Rhum   Venetian Meringues
Neapolitan Creams   Pineapple Creams
Italian Creams   Strawberry Creams
Lemon Jelly   Cherry Jelly
Victoria Jelly   Mildred Jelly
Millefruit Cakes   Madrid Cakes   Princess Cakes
Chocolate Pastry   Duchess Pastry

Stilton, Cheddar, and Cream Cheeses
Biscuits   Butter
Dessert

The soup was hot, the remainder of the dinner cold; five hundred, including ladies, sat down, and the repast was served in a large tent; and plenty of that favourite brand of champagne of his father's (Sir Edward Lawson) 'Pol Roger,' 1874, accompanied the entertainment, and a noble baron of beef was carved from an elevated daïs on the side of the tent.

One of the most delightful dinners I ever sat down to was at the hospitable table of that prince of good fellows, Mr. Henry Brassey (alas! now no more), at his beautiful seat, Preston Hall, Kent. A few of his personal friends had been invited on the eve of his sale of short-horns, and besides there were about eighteen guests in the house; and it is needless to say that this exquisite dinner was accompanied by the choicest vintages, and the Lafite claret and glorious old port will never be forgotten. The dining-room and all its appointments left nothing to be desired. The mansion itself, equal to anything I have ever seen, was built a few years since regardless of expense by the late Mr. Betts. It stands in matchless gardens, with avenues and groves of choice roses and a lovely park on the banks of the Medway, and the whole forms a scene only to be found in Old England, and leaves behind a memory of hearty welcome and perfect urbanity rarely equalled.

These records of good living would not be complete without giving the menu of a real Mansion House dinner. The Lord Mayor, the late Sir Andrew Lusk, in the year 1874, on March 20, gave a banquet to the Chambers of Commerce and Agriculture, and as one of the members of the latter I had the honour of being invited. The form and ceremony preceding the dinner were stately and appropriate. The band of the Coldstream Guards played during dinner, and a most pleasing vocal concert interspersed the toasts of the evening and made a very enjoyable entertainment. After the banquet the guests partook of coffee, tea, &c., and lounged and chatted in the corridors and anterooms, whilst cigars and liqueurs were handed round. The Egyptian Hall was used for the dining-room, and is a most magnificent apartment. The massive civic plate, the splendid adornment of the tables, the excellence of the viands, and quality of the wines formed a *tout ensemble* worthy of the first magistrate of the first city in the world, and I trust the day is far distant when this grand corporation will cease to display its magnificent hospitality to all visitors, whether from home or abroad.

POTAGES
Tortue et Tortue claire

POISSONS
Truite de Spey à la Chevalier
Escalopes de Soles aux fines Herbes
Saumon à la Tartare
Turbot—Sauce de Homard

ENTRÉES
Croustade de Mauviettes à la Parisienne
Ris d'Agneau à la Villeroi

RELEVÉS
Chapon braisé à la Périgueux
Petits Poulets au Macédoine
Jambon d'York   Selle de Mouton
Quartier d'Agneau

RÔTS
Oisons   Dindonneaux piqués   Cercelles

ENTREMETS
Crevettes en buisson
Flan de Fruits à la Crème
Gelées claires   Bavarois aux Raisins
Crème aux Ananas
Meringues à la Crème   Beignets à la Séville

RELEVÉS
Poudings à la Nesselrode   Petits Soufflés glacés
Caviar

When the Royal Agricultural Society of England held their annual show at Kilburn, in 1879, I again had the pleasure of dining at the Mansion House. On that occasion the Lord Mayor, Sir Charles Whetham, entertained the Prince of Wales (the president), the council of the Society, and the judges, of whom I was one, as I judged the foreign cattle. This banquet was even a more *recherché* repast than the other, and when the loving-cup was passed round to the distinguished guests, and the sonorous sounds of Mr. Toole, the toast-master, gave the solemn pledge to them, it was a sight long to be remembered by all who witnessed it.

When I was at the Vienna Exhibition, an old friend of mine, Mr. Joseph Robinson, was there with his family, and one day he took a carriage and pair of horses and invited me to accompany him on an excursion to the Kalenberg, a lofty hill overlooking the valley of the Danube and the city of Vienna at its feet. It reminded us of the Thames and Richmond, and it boasted a restaurant considered the best out of Vienna. The view was magnificent. Mr. Robinson left it to his courier to order a luncheon for us. I give the bill seriatim.

BILL FOR FIVE PERSONS

	Fl.	K.
Suppe		60
Fische (Trout)	4	90
Beefstecks	6	30
Corfeil (Cauliflower) . . .	3	
Spargel (Asparagus) . . .	6	
Backhut (grilled Fowl) . .	3	60
Salade		60
Gardinette, one plate of fruit .	3	60
Kafe (small) glasses . . .	1	80
Wine, 1 Bottle of Hock, and Café	4	50
Brod	1	
Service	1	
	41	10

It was a very ordinary entertainment, served in a very inferior style to a Richmond or Greenwich repast, and the charges were enormous. The amount in English money came to over 4*l.*, which for a slight luncheon and one bottle of common ordinary hock was therefore over 16*s.* each. It will be observed that the thieves had cast it up 5 florins, or 10*s.*, wrong against us, which we did not observe until we had returned to Vienna. In the Exhibition grounds, at the Swedish restaurant, my kind friend, Mr. Juland Dannefelt, the chief Consul for Sweden, now in London, gave a splendid entertainment to Mr. Cunliffe-Owen, Count Schwartz Schenborn, and about twenty-four others, at which I was present, and the viands and wines were superb.

Whilst recording events relating to gastronomy, and showing the different varieties of entertainments with their respective menus, I cannot quote from printed and other documents of earlier times, with the exception of one which has already appeared in print, but is in such contrast to these preceding that I am tempted to produce it. The dinner was given at the White Hart, Aylesbury, on September 13, 1815, to Lord Blaney, by the officers of the Bucks Yeomanry.

Each course was placed on the table complete, with sauces, vegetables, side-dishes or entrées, with the joints and everything carved and served from the table. This was considered at that time one of the most *recherché* dinners ever given at an inn, and by a new young man-cook, just fresh from one of the colleges in Oxford. There were twenty guests who partook of the dinner.

FIRST COURSE
Turtle Soup
Potatoes
Lobster Sauce   Turbot   Lobster Sauce
Potatoes
Turtle Soup

SECOND COURSE
Boiled Fowls
Haricot Mutton   Beef Olives
Oyster Sauce
Turnips and Carrots
Tongue
Greens   Saddle of Lamb   Stewed Pigeons
Salad
Veal Olives   Boiled Leg of Pork   French Beans
Potatoes   Pease Pudding
Tremlong of Beef   Roast Fowls   Cauliflower

THIRD COURSE
Brace of Birds
Sweet Sauce   Hare   Bread Sauce
Potatoes   Flowers   Potatoes
Hare
Bread Sauce   Brace of Birds   Sweet Sauce

FOURTH COURSE
Gooseberry Pie
Jelly   Baked Apple Pudding   Blanc-mange
Custards   Plum Pie   Apricot Tart
Apricot Tart   Boiled Plum Pudding   Custards
Blanc-mange   Fruit in Jelly
Turtle Punch
Port, Sherry, Claret, Champagne

The cost of this dinner, including wine, was thirty shillings each.

CHAPTER XI

Journey to Bordeaux—Orléans—Châteaux de Blois, Chambord, Chenonceaux, d'Amboise, &c.—St. Cross and the Dole—Marshal Saxe—'Les Landes'—Biarritz—Sea-bathing—Fontarabia—Pau—Bordeaux—Foreign opinion of cattle, &c.—Letters from Moët and Johnston.

IN the year 1868 I had some spare time after harvest, and determined to pay my long contemplated visit into the wine districts of France, especially to the claret and champagne countries, and in the second week in September started with two young friends to see the beauties of the west coast of France, too much neglected by British tourists. No part of the Continent ought to be more interesting to the English people than this district, hallowed as it is in the minds of all Englishmen by the battlefields of Crécy and Agincourt. Here, too, were wrought the doughty deeds of our glorious Black Prince, and here are the tombs of many of our Plantagenet kings and queens at Fontevrault. Here, too, we mourn the memory of Orléans and the sad ending of 'La Pucelle.' Coming to later times we read of the gallant deeds of our Peninsular army under Wellington, when he passed the Adour in 1814, and invaded France. The scenery is picturesque and historically interesting, such as the valley of the Loire and its lovely castles, its Château d'Amboise, its Châteaux

Chenonceaux and Gomont, rich in the memories of Diane de Poictiers and of the Medicis, and above all that most interesting and most beautiful of the *châteaux* in Europe of the Renaissance period, Heidelberg alone excepted—I mean the Château de Chambord. When one thinks of the historic towns, the stately cathedrals, and the picturesque mansions which are to be seen in this beautiful part of France, at Orléans, Blois, Tours, Poictiers, and Angoulême, it is wonderful to me how few Englishmen take the trouble to visit it. We left London by morning mail, and arrived in Paris the same evening, slept at the Grand Hôtel du Louvre, and about ten o'clock A.M. started for Blois, where we arrived in good time in the afternoon. This fine old town is interesting to us as being the birthplace of our King Stephen, and also of Henry de Blois, who founded the Hospital of St. Cross, near Winchester. Henry de Blois built the beautiful Norman church attached to the hospital, where to this day a curious custom is kept up. At the buttery-hatch in the postern gate they give to all comers a piece of bread and a horn of beer, which on several occasions I have myself demanded and received with many poor wayfarers. On one occasion I saw a sorely tired young man, who was travelling from Portsmouth to London, call there, dusty and worn out, and ask for this bounty, and when he had finished his beer I heard him thank God and the noble founder who had given him that welcome refreshment. Little did he think or know that 700 years ago a now long-forgotten Norman, intimately bound up with the history of this country, had endowed that excellent charity, and

VISIT TO BLOIS AND ITS CHÂTEAU   111

granted him that dole. I thought of this when walking through the streets of this mediæval old French town, and was gratified at the recollection of the link which connected me with the history of the past. We stayed at the Hôtel d'Angleterre, the best in the place ; a good *table d'hôte*, a tolerably good bedroom, but the hotel sadly deficient in all those sanitary comforts that Englishmen are accustomed to. Why is it that there should be such an utter ignorance of the commonest principles of sanitation as exists in almost all hotels in every city in Europe, and private houses also? Surely the constant visits of thousands of English men and women should by this time have had some effect in blotting out this foul nuisance ; but, except in some of the modern hotels, there has been but little improvement during the past thirty years. Our bedroom windows overlooked the Loire, and a fine bridge crosses the river close to our hotel. We visited the noble old *château*, which had been lately restored by the Emperor Napoleon III. ; it is a grand pile and very picturesque. You are shown the room where the Duc de Guise was murdered, and many other points of interest. In the courtyard is a remarkable turret, which incloses a staircase of considerable width, and which leads up to each story of the building. As this turret is outside, and forms a fine architectural feature of the structure, I thought it an admirable suggestion for modern architects, who are often troubled about their staircases, which take up a considerable amount of room that could be otherwise utilised ; I had noticed this feature in several other places on the Continent. The cathedral is a fine specimen of thirteenth century Gothic, but in sad need of repair. On visiting the market-place, which is surrounded by very quaint old buildings, we bought twenty-five peaches for half a franc, and distributed them amongst the children, who were highly delighted with 'Milor Anglais;' we also bought a large and most excellent melon for 2½ centimes! A large fair was being held in the adjoining streets, with tents and booths, where every sort of merchandise was being sold. At one stall a man spoke English remarkably well, and his wares consisted of stationery and fancy articles. We bought of him some blotting-paper, which was very dear; he told us he was rarely asked for it, as everyone used sand over their writing, shaken out of a little caster like pepper.

One of my young friends was so struck with the blandishments of a very pretty girl that he was persuaded by her to buy a not very romantic article, viz. *a sponge*; let me hope it did not wipe out the memory of her bewitching eyes, which looked so imploringly at him, as he concluded his very dear purchase in a delicious jargon of English and French. We distributed in a succession of scrambles whole handfuls of sweetmeats to the crowd of children who followed us. On walking over the bridge, we found each side of the footway was devoted to the sale of hardware—pots, kettles, pans, old chains, hooks, nails, and tools were the chief articles. On our return to the hotel we engaged a carriage for the morning to take us to the Château de Chambord. After an early and excellent breakfast we started for this far-famed *château*. Our road lay through a level and not

THE CHÂTEAU DE CHAMBORD

very picturesque country, the greater part of our journey —about eight miles—being devoted to the culture of the vine. These vines are well pruned, trained, and cared for, and the fruit was just changing colour, and ripening. The grapes were handsome, and the bunches large. The wines made on the Loire are much inferior to those on the Garonne, which is the true claret district. This Loire wine is chiefly drunk at dinner in most of the hotels in Paris. It is of a good stout character, but wanting in the delicacy of the wines of Bordeaux.

At length we arrived at our destination, when *the château par excellence* burst upon our sight; it is built in a rather low-lying district, and is surrounded by a deep, thick forest, well stocked with game. I have never yet seen a building in my opinion so remarkable as this, as a specimen of the highest development of the Renaissance style. I am not architect enough to describe it in professional terms, but can say it is the most ornate, picturesque, and for its purpose the best adapted building I have ever seen. It was built by Francis I. in the time of our Tudor kings, but the style was very different from our English style of the period. From the centre rises a tower, or corona, this latter feature completing or crowning the pile. *Finis coronat opus.* Both inside and outside the building the prevailing ornament is the 'Salamander,' the cognisance of Francis, which adorns the cornices, the capitals of the columns, and indeed every place where it could be introduced. It certainly is a design eminently adapted for the purpose, and is duly enshrined in the palace. To me the most striking part of the building is the grand staircase;

this is placed in the centre, or at the intersection of the main body of the *château*, which is of vast extent. This staircase is built spirally; there is a broad flight of steps winding upwards, and another of the same size winding downwards, like a corkscrew, so that the guests ascending are prevented meeting those descending, and yet they are in full view of each other, the carving of the balustrades and stonework being very open. One can picture the scene in the days of Francis: the courtiers with their velvet doublets, trunk hose, and silk stockings of gay colours, accompanied by their dames in brilliant and rich brocades, with ruffs and hanging sleeves, trimmed with elaborate lace, ascending and descending this double staircase. It must have presented a most brilliant picture. The *château* was never quite completed, and has been long unoccupied. The history of this architectural wonder is curious. At the beginning of the seventeenth century it was given by the King of France to Marshal Saxe, who made it his residence. When he was no longer able to take the field, and the gout and other infirmities compelled the old warrior to keep his room, it was his custom to sit at one of the windows, and from that elevated position to put through their manœuvres a regiment of cavalry, which had been allotted to him by the king, and was quartered on the premises, and this he continued to do until his death. When the Emperor Napoleon seized the crown, after some of his greatest exploits, he gave the *château* and the estate around it to Marshal Berthier, and some time after the restoration of the Bourbons the widow of the marshal died, and the property was put up to auction. The whole of the surrounding district clubbed together, being intensely Royalist, and raised a large subscription, and bought it, and presented it to the Comte de Chambord, the rightful heir to the monarchy.

In the afternoon we started for Bordeaux, stopping *en route* at Tours to enable us to see the town and the cathedral, which latter is a very interesting structure, with a remarkably imposing Gothic tower. The bridge crossing the Loire is a fine one, and the view both up and down the stream very picturesque. We passed Poictiers, the line crossing the site of that glorious battle, so intimately connected with the history of the Black Prince; we passed by Angoulême, and arrived at Bordeaux at night or early in the morning, and went to the Hôtel d'Angleterre. After breakfast we called on my friends, Messrs. Nathaniel Johnston and Sons, at the Pavé de Chartrons, and were received most kindly; and the head of the firm, a fine specimen of the 'old English gentleman,' told me we were too early for the vintage, which it was my desire to see, and said he would give us a little tour to occupy our time for a week, so as to be ready for the vintage, which would then be in full swing. By his suggestion we took our departure for Bayonne, where we arrived the next day, passing through that part of France called 'Les Landes,' a dreary flat plain of sand, which a few years since was a desert, but had during the last three governments been rendered of considerable commercial value. The whole district for many miles had been planted with fir trees, which had just become useful, as they were large enough for the production of resin and turpentine. The method of securing this product is to give the growing trunk of the tree a sharp blow with an axe, cutting a slice of the bark nearly off. This is then bent down, and a tin vessel holding nearly a pint is hung on by a wire, and the resin drops into it as it exudes from the tree. A very considerable income is now derived from the district, which was formerly utterly barren. The country is covered with furze, or gorse, as an undergrowth where it is not planted with trees, and it is very difficult to walk over in consequence. Numerous flocks of sheep are kept here to feed on the young shoots and sparse herbage, and the shepherds in charge cannot get near their flocks because of the sharp prickles which abound; they therefore go on stilts, which not only save their legs, but enable them to see over the flat district on which their sheep are grazing. It is very amusing to see these men at rest in the bushes; they have a long staff in their hands and a strap over their shoulders, and between their shoulder-blades is a leathern belt, with an iron or wooden cup, into which they insert the end of the staff, and lean against it, making, with their stretched-out stilts, a sort of tripod, and it is not uncommon to see them thus resting and going to sleep in perfect security.

Bayonne is a very handsome town, and is historically interesting owing to the gallant sortie made by its garrison when the town was besieged by our troops under Wellington. We stayed a night at the Hôtel de France, a very comfortable and excellently managed house. In the morning we started for Biarritz, and whilst there enjoyed ourselves immensely with the sea-bathing. The manners and customs rather shocked our modesty, and created many a laugh then, and for years afterwards, in recounting our experiences. There was a sort of casino or bathing verandah, with small dressing rooms, where I was furnished with a distinguished costume, like to that of Grimaldi, the celebrated clown, of broad scarlet and white stripes, with a full frill or collar round my throat, the same frilling round my arms near the shoulders, another round my waist, and very full frillings above my knees; in this costume, with my two companions, in different colours, we marched over the sands, about 150 yards, into 'the Bay of Biscay, oh!' From the building all along the shore ladies in gorgeous costumes and gaily ornamented head-dresses were being escorted into the sea by their male companions, and some of them, who rather hesitated to venture amongst the billows, were led into the water by big, hirsute fellows in waterproof costumes, and sou'-westers like North Sea fishermen, who left them when safely in the water. My first encounter when I was disporting myself amongst the waves was with a big, fat Frenchwoman, who rolled fairly over me, knocking me down; we both sprang up, and she spluttered out, with the sea-water pouring down her face, 'Pardon, monsieur!' and rushed away bursting with laughter. The water was delightfully warm and most enjoyable; after nearly half an hour's gambols we returned across the sands, our costumes presenting a rather more draggled appearance than when we entered the sea.

We had an excellent *table d'hôte* at the Hôtel de France, where we were staying, and in the morning left for a short trip into Spain. We passed through Hendeya, to the frontier town of Irun, where we stopped for a few hours to enable us to visit one of the most interesting places I ever saw. After passing Irun, the railway threads its way at the foot of the Pyrenees, and suddenly curves round a spur of the mountains, when a scene burst on my view which I shall never forget; close to the line was the sea, forming the landlocked harbour of Passages, the water being the most intense blue, and on the opposite side of the harbour was the picturesque old Moorish town of Fontarabia, ' where Charlemagne and all his peerage fell by Fontarabia.' At the back of the town rose the Pyrenees, with their glorious purple tints, blending harmoniously with the rich yellow or burnt sienna colours of the old cathedral, the castle, and the dilapidated walls of the ancient fortifications, the whole being reflected in the deep blue of the sea, which almost washes the foot of the town. It was a glorious view, and of the greatest interest to me.

Wishing to make a closer inspection of the architecture of these fine old structures, we ordered at Irun a carriage to be prepared; when all was ready I could not help noticing the pair of horses, attached by rope harness to the vehicle supplied to us—a black and a flea-bitten grey, poor-looking beasts, all skin and bone of the finest quality and texture; their manes and tales were of long and silky softness, and at first to me they were a riddle; but as they rattled along at full gallop, up steep hills and down the roads, I could see they were of some pure breed, though sorely in need of condition. I soon discovered that many horses of the district are of *pure Arab descent*, staunchly bred by the Moors, who once were the masters of Spain. When admiring the architectural beauties of Fontarabia I was rather at cross-purposes with a local guide, who seeing me very interested in Charlemagne and the Moors, and that I was eager to see the actual fields where the great fights went on—the fellow led me, with a wild torrent of enthusiasm, to some indentations in the masonry of the old castle, and proudly pointed out to me *imbedded in the walls the very cannon-balls that were fired during the war.* I need not say he was describing the struggles and last efforts of Don Carlos, and thus destroyed all my romantic ideas of 'The Cid' and the dominion of the Moors in Spain. We went on to St. Sebastian, and were greatly pleased with this Spanish town, and especially with the great fortress which was stormed by the invincible Peninsular army of Wellington; it seems incredible how our soldiers could have scaled the heights, and stormed the citadel, the rock on which the fortress stands being almost perpendicular; our losses were tremendous, and it was indeed a melancholy sight to witness the spot where so many hundred officers and men of that *Nulli Secundus* army lie buried. After seeing the town, we returned and went on to Pau— the loveliest place I ever beheld. To those who have not visited this enchanting spot, I can never give in words a description of the exquisite views from the old castle where Henri IV. was born, and where his cradle is still shown. The Pyrenees have a charm entirely their own. The rich warm colour of the rocks, and the soil of the mountains, when clothed with purple heather, and bathed in the glow of an autumnal evening sun, form a scene of unrivalled beauty; we stayed at the 'Hôtel des Postes,' a house renowned for its cuisine; we had an excellent dinner, and I have not forgotten a wonderful dish, as an *entremet*, of peach fritters, which was delicious. In the evening we were aroused by a cry of 'Fire!' and a crowd soon collected round the burning house, which was very near the *château*, but by the efforts of the military, who were called out, the *château* escaped.

We took a drive through the mountains to the 'Pic du Midi,' and were really enchanted with their beauty; we passed through the village of Jurançon, famed for its wine, which was white, and said to be *très fort*, but as we were English bred, and inured to strong ale and port and sherry, we did not think much of it, either for strength or flavour.

After another day spent in the enjoyment of this lovely scenery, we returned *viâ* Orthez—another scene of the triumphs of our Peninsular veterans—and then by Dax, where we were shamefully robbed at the refreshment department of the station, by paying extreme rates for bad food and execrable wine. We then returned to Bayonne, and the next day arrived again at Bordeaux; in the evening we attended the grand opera, and heard 'La Dame Blanche.' I think it is one of Boïeldieu's works. The performance was good, but not quite first class. The opera house is splendid, and is considered one of the handsomest in Europe.

Our English ideas were not much impressed with the method of farming on the Continent, and generally we are apt to despise the opinions and practice of foreigners in their selection of breeding stock, and to boast of our superiority; but they have reasons which, on investigation, I found were of practical utility. For instance, we find fault with the long legs and elongated snouts of their pigs, and praise our short-legged and short-snouted heavy-jowled Berkshires; but I found from one gentleman from Hungary that his pigs roamed the forests, especially in the winter, when the snow was on the ground, and if they had short legs the severity of the weather caused injury to the teats of the sows, and the length of the snout enabled them to grub up the acorns and roots in the forests, and that whatever shortness of snouts they begin with, in a few years the snout becomes elongated. So also it is with their cattle. In most countries on the Continent the bullocks and cows are used as much for beasts of burthen as they are for beef and milk, therefore they have heavy shoulders, thick hides, and strong legs. The distaste also for fat mutton, especially amongst the French, causes them to keep the Merino and Southdowns—or, as they call them, 'Race Jonas Webb'—and so get plenty of lean meat and short fine wool, as against our Shropshires, Lincolns, and Leicesters, with wool of long staple.

In giving a slight sketch of the journey to visit my excellent friends, Messrs. Nathaniel Johnston and Sons, at Bordeaux, and Messrs. Moët and Chandon, of Epernay, it may not be uninteresting to quote letters I received from these two eminent firms the year after I had visited them, viz. 1869. This was the year preceding the great Franco-German War, and it shows how little these great authorities thought of the volcano that was about to burst on them within a short year after the letters were written. Mr. Nathaniel Johnston, after speaking of the arrival of some valuable poultry I had sent him to Bordeaux, and admiring the Aylesbury ducks, says :—

> I have just received one of your County papers relative to the shows in which you figured prominently, and also one in which I read a capital and straightforward speech of yours. Would to heaven we could have such meetings carried on with equally good feeling in this country! Our legislation for the last seventeen years, ever since the appearance of the Emperor on the stage, had prohibited anything like political meetings even at electioneering times, and now that public feeling is forcing the administration to give way in some slight degree in this respect, the speaking portion of the community, like schoolboys let free after undue confinement, go wild in the theories they propound, much to the annoyance of moderate and well-thinking persons of all opinions. I only hope the administration will not be frightened, but will allow full freedom for all opinions to manifest themselves; it is the only way of finding an antidote to the poisonous doctrines held forth.

At the time I was visiting Mr. Johnston, his eldest son was canvassing the constituency of the county of Bordeaux as its representative in Parliament as an Imperialist, and was returned by a majority of about 1,200.

Mr. Auban Moët, of Epernay, wrote at the same date :—

> Mr. Moët, my father-in-law, who is unfortunately very unwell, just now requested me to answer your kind letter. Mr. Moët read with great pleasure of the success of your cattle sale, and went

over the contents of the 'Bucks Herald' with interest. Personally we are largely and exclusively vine-growers, and meddle very little with cattle; and such is the case with nearly everyone in our country, as the vine requires very little if any manure. I am aware of two gentlemen only in this neighbourhood who are addicted to farming—the Marquis de Montmort and Baron Kiogener, but I am afraid the very high prices fetched by your short-horn cattle would deter both from trying the experiment. The Champagne is a very dry country, meadows few and not extensive, grass scarce and hay very dear; horned cattle do not thrive here, the country is much more favourable for sheep. This year's vintage (1869) is very inconsiderable; the wine will be very good. Undoubtedly the 1868 is one of the very best years to be numbered in the present century; it stands on a par with 1822, 1834, and 1848. The politics of France are brightening. The Emperor's health is better, and our prospects also. The time of entire liberty we went through has brought to the light such an amount of nonsense, ignorance, and depravity, that the sound part of the nation has shrunk away with disgust from the self-named *irreconcilables*. The effervescing wit of France seems to be sobering down to sense and calmness. Yet we are much in want of some of your good old sporting English qualities. You may sometimes be quarrelling about ways and means, but with you the very principles of society, civilisation, and government are already settled.

These were the opinions then held, and in a little more than a year all was over!

CHAPTER XII

George Stephenson and Delmé Radcliffe on Railways — Vienna Exhibition — My cattle — Nuremberg — Albert Dürer — Sir A. de Rothschild — Voyage down the Danube — Blondel and Richard Cœur de Lion — A sword-swallower — The Emperor Franz Joseph — The Crown Prince Rudolph — Baron Albert de Rothschild — Procrastination — The Tyrol — Salzburg — Judging at Agricultural Shows — Manchester — Drying hay — Churns and dairy appliances — Kilburn — Foreign cattle — Ensilage — Altona — Schleswig-Holstein — H. Corbet.

MORE than fifty years ago—now 1893—railways had begun to make themselves known as the future means of locomotion through the country, and I well remember old George Stephenson being at my father's house. At that time I had left school about two years, and I was taken into his sitting-room to hear him tell my father some of the early history of his career. His companion was Mr. Bidder, who a few years before had been taken round the country and exhibited as the wonderful calculating boy. Mr. Stephenson was then making and suggesting many branch lines in connection with the then London and Birmingham Railway, and his visit to Aylesbury was to obtain land that might be made into a wharf for the sale of his Clay Cross coal, a valuable seam of which had been discovered in making the well-known Clay Cross tunnel on the Midland line. My father let him about two acres of land, where his wharf was established, and the coal was sold there for many years. I have the lease now ; it was for fourteen years, and was signed with three most eminent names : George Stephenson, Carr - Glyn (afterwards Lord Wolverton), Joshua Walmesley. I remember George Stephenson combated the idea that horse labour would be abolished, and said that so greatly would trade and manufactures increase that horses would be required to convey this increase to the various stations on the line and the ports in connection with them, and that, consequently, more horses would be required than ever. The coach proprietors and post-masters would suffer greatly, but even that trade would in time somewhat recover.

It is well known, and by none better than myself, that the main line into the north was originally to go down from London *viâ* Uxbridge, Amersham, and Aylesbury, now occupied by the Metropolitan Railway. Every landowner on the line opposed George Stephenson's scheme, so the Countess of Bridgwater sent for him, and asked : 'Why don't you follow the line of the Grand Junction Canal, through my property at Berkhamstead and Tring ? ' and using a most expressive term, she continued : 'The land is already *gashed* by the Canal, and if you take that course you will have no severance to pay, it will disarm opposition, and the position of the locks will be some guide to you in your levels.' Mr. Stephenson took her advice, and the present London and North-Western Railway line is the consequence.

So little was known even by men of intelligence as to the probable effects of the introduction of railways into England that I find so high a sporting authority as

Mr. Delmé Radcliffe, in his book on the noble science of fox-hunting, written in 1830, lamenting the probable results of the introduction of railways, and saying :

> How far this trebly accursed revolution of railroads may affect the breeding of hunters and foxhounds it is impossible to say ; and when all the inns and roadside houses are tenantless and gone to decay, and the present occupiers being lost in the abyss of inevitable ruin, when not only posting, post-horses, and even turnpikes have become matters of history, and we bewail the beauties of the old parks spoiled ; and when we consider the magnitude of the convulsion which this mighty railway delusion will effect—the thousands of human beings thrown out of employ, the incalculable diminution in the number of horses, and the consequent deficiency in the demand for agricultural produce, and the enormous loss to the revenue by the abolition of the post-horse duties—and when we reflect on these things we cannot but wonder at the blindness that has countenanced the growth of this monster, which will soon eat up the vitals of those by whom it was fostered.

In 1873 the Great Exhibition for all nations was held at Vienna, and I was anxious that England should be represented. Accordingly, together with some other short-horn and sheep breeders, we made up a fairly good entry. I entered a very good short-horn bull, for which I obtained the first prize. On his being shown to the Emperor Franz Joseph, the latter requested that he might be led out for his inspection, and he expressed his admiration more especially at his size, considering that his age was only a year and ten months. The bull was Royal Geneva, and a good specimen of a Bates and Knightley animal. I had arranged with Messrs. Cook for the transport of all the exhibits, which were sent *viâ* Harwich and Antwerp. I myself and a few others started two days afterwards with a desire to see some noted places on the way, and, as I had been more than once on the Rhine, I pushed on to Nuremberg, which I had long desired to see, as being the home of Albrecht Dürer, the cradle of his genius, and the receptacle of much of his artistic works. This city far exceeded my most sanguine expectations ; I think it is nearly the most interesting town in Europe, being only surpassed by our own classic Oxford. I went into a restaurant which I was told Hans Sachs was accustomed to frequent, and sat on the same bench, at the same table, that this noted poet used. Further, I was served with the same description of food, with the same pattern of dishes, plates, knives, and Black Jack out of which to drink the same class of beer that used to be served to him.

There are famous specimens of Albrecht Dürer's metal work and wood and stone carving in the streets and the churches ; and the torture chambers and diabolical implements of punishment were too horrible to be described. The butchers' market and manufactories of toys are worth seeing.. I was staying at a very interesting hotel, the Baierischer Hof, and found that Sir Anthony and Lady de Rothschild were there on their return from Vienna to London, and as Sir Anthony was a near neighbour of mine, and one of the commissioners for the Exhibition, I had hoped to have his assistance at the show. When I called on him in the morning he was astonished at seeing me, but greeted me most cordially, and asked what brought me so far from the Vale of Aylesbury. I soon explained to him that my cattle and other live stock, with that of others of his own acquaintance, had been sent on to Vienna, and I found he was much pleased, as he was a good farmer and took the greatest interest in agriculture. I told him how much I regretted his absence from the Exhibition, as I had hoped to have had his assistance on my arrival. He said he would give me a letter of introduction to his cousin, Baron Albert de Rothschild, who would be able to do a great deal more for me than he could possibly do himself; so after breakfasting, and giving me strict injunctions to be sure and see the ballet of 'Fantanitza' at the opera, and giving me the letter, we parted, he on his way to London, and I by way of Regensburg (Ratisbon), where there is a fine mediæval cathedral, by rail to Passau. Here I took steamer down the Danube to Linz, and thence to Vienna. I was much impressed with the grandeur of the river, and the places of interest we passed; at one place, where the steamer touched at a landing stage, an old castle was near, and a window was pointed out to me as the one at which Blondel discovered the lion-hearted king, his master, Richard Cœur de Lion. I was much amused by a real black 'Nigger' who was on board the steamer, who told me he had come direct from England alone. He spoke English well and told me he was a *swordswallower*, and had been engaged to go to the Exhibition; he knew nothing of the language, but was to be met at one of the landing stages on the river to perform at some tea-gardens for a week or two. He told me that on the night before, when at Linz, he had strolled over the river to the barracks, and asked one of the soldiers for his sword bayonet for a minute, and immediately had

THE EMPEROR AND PRINCE RUDOLPH

put it down his throat. The man thought he was committing suicide, till he pulled it from his throat again, and handed it politely to the soldier, amidst shouts of laughter, and exclamations of astonishment. A crowd soon collected round him, and the officers begged him to show his powers to them, which he did, and they were bewildered at his feats, and a subscription was made for him.

My kind friend Mr. (now Sir) Cunliffe-Owen had taken apartments for me and Lord Chesham and his daughter at the Römischer Kaiser, one of the noted old hotels in the city, situated in the 'Freyung,' near the Ringstrasse. The Emperor with a great number of the leading nobles of the Court, came to the opening of the Exhibition, and I had the honour of being introduced to him, and the next day his son Prince Rudolph was brought by Count Schwartz Schenborn, with a desire that I should take him round and show him the English cattle, sheep, and pigs. I did so, and explained to him the peculiarities of the different breeds. I found him a most intelligent and delightful youth; he was then about seventeen years of age, and spoke English fairly well. It is a sad memory to me, when I think of the great promise of this young prince, and his sad and tragic end about twelve years afterwards. I heard an interesting anecdote of him when he was about thirteen years old. He was coming out of a shop in Vienna with his tutor, when a gentleman met him, and being much struck with his appearance, and utterly unconscious of his position, patted him on the shoulder and said, 'What is your name, my little gentleman?' The prince said, 'My

K

father and mother call me Rudolph, but everyone else, *your Royal Highness!*' I heard in all quarters of the extreme popularity of the Emperor, and his beautiful Empress, of whom I have vivid remembrances whilst hunting in the vale of Aylesbury. I found my letter of introduction to Baron Albert de Rothschild of great value; nothing could exceed his kindness, and the consideration shown me; and he gave me his box at the opera to see the ballet of 'Fantanitza,' which happened to be the night of the visit of the Emperor and Empress, with the Czar of Russia, Dagmar, the Cesarevna, the King of Saxony, and nearly all the Court, and such a brilliant assembly I never saw before. Baron Albert came up from his stall, and pointed out to us all the celebrities present. My agricultural friends and myself managed to sell all the live stock we took over, though at prices far below what we could have made in England, but the fear we had of bringing back cattle disease made us get rid of them. One of the sights which most astonished the attendants on the foreign and native cattle was when William Day, Lord Chesham's shepherd, was shearing one of Mr. Robert Russell's Kentish long-wools; when the fleece rolled off its back, in snowy whiteness, and was found to weigh over fourteen pounds, they could scarcely believe it, as the fleeces of the Merinos, which are the prevalent sheep of those countries, would not weigh more than five or six pounds.

Great difficulty had been experienced in getting together a jury of Englishmen. The jury consisted of eleven sections, and one Englishman was expected to be on each. Lord Chesham and myself were made

AUSTRIAN OPINION OF BRITISH AGRICULTURE 131

'experts' or referees, should any difficulty arise. I have been rather explicit in mentioning this on account of an incident which happened the night before the Exhibition opened, which I hope I may relate with pardonable pride, as it involved the highest compliment I ever heard paid to English agriculture. When the jury were assembled together, the president addressed us, in German, telling us our duties; but I was fortunate in having sitting opposite to me a Mr. Zoeppritz, a Bavarian, who was well known in England, and who spoke our language, and he interpreted to me and my fellow-jurors sitting near the gist of the president's remarks. After a long address he concluded thus : ' But if any of you are in any doubt as to your decisions give way to the English judges, as they know so much more about agriculture than all of us together, that you cannot do wrong in agreeing with them.' As there were Austrians, Germans, Russians, French, Poles, Italians, Swedes, Belgians, and Swiss amongst us, my fellow-judges and myself felt much flattered ; and I found that practically the president's advice in the main was followed.

I discovered a remarkable peculiarity among the foreigners I met on the Continent, viz. that they attach so little importance to punctuality in keeping appointments. They have no idea of our English habits, and I believe that our rule of 'Never put off till to-morrow what you can do to-day,' is travestied by ' Never do to-day what you can put off till the week after next.'

I left the beautiful city of Vienna with regret, after wishing my kind friends adieu, and was much gratified with my visit and the sights I had seen. I returned viâ Linz, where I left the main route and passed on by Gmunden through the Tyrol, the beauties of which most picturesque of countries I shall not attempt to describe. Then by the Salzkammergut, Salzburg, Augsburg, and Munich, at which places we stayed for a time, and so by Strasburg and Paris to London. I returned home improved, I hope, by my study of Eastern European manners and customs, and with a fixed belief in the superiority of England in every department of agriculture.

Amongst my most pleasing recollections are those relating to agriculture, and I hope I may be pardoned if the incidents I shall relate should be deemed too egotistical. I began farming on my own account in 1853, and that year was as disastrous from the continued rain and floods as was this year of grace 1893 from the drought, and the flocks of the country were then decimated by the liver rot. I lost nearly 250 sheep in six months, either dead, or sold to escape death, at a few shillings a head. Nothing daunted, I drained the farm by the assistance of my landlord, and in three years there was no farm better adapted for sheep, except that in winter the land was too soft for the flock to be as dry and comfortable as they would have been on the Cotswold Hills. I have had the honour of being appointed judge at several of the meetings of the Royal Agricultural Society of England. Once on a memorable occasion, when the show was held at Old Trafford, near Manchester, in conjunction with two others I was appointed to adjudicate on the miscellaneous implements, and the council particularly drew our attention to an apparatus for drying wet hay, and damaged corn in the sheaf, as illustrating a most important principle. After an exhaustive trial we found that, by passing a current of dry or heated air through a cylinder, with an Archimedean screw inside it, which carried the hay onwards, we succeeded in drying it. It struck me that it was advisable to call in some *experts* to assist us in our decision, and I carried in my arms a lot of this dried provender, and put it before some cattle and horses, *and not one of them would eat it*. I then tried it with sheep, with the same results; in the end we gave way to our assistant judges, and passed the apparatus over without a prize. At this meeting we were asked to look at some hives of bees, which we declined to do, as they did not come under the head of agricultural implements, but the exhibitor seriously and stoutly maintained that bees were carriers of agricultural produce, and were a sort of wagons and carts for carrying the products of the field. Some years after it was rightly deemed necessary to give prizes for bees and honey-making appliances. Amongst the judges at this meeting I have a lively recollection of Mr. (now Sir Frederick) Bramwell, who was the life and soul of our party, which numbered about twenty-four, and whose witty conversation kept us all in good humour. I also awarded the prizes for dairy implements at the show of the society at Oxford, and it is impossible to describe the great value of competition in this particular department. It would be invidious to give names, but in corroboration of my views I mention the following. Some three or four years after the Oxford show, I met an exhibitor who was, I think, second or third in churns, and we had given the first prize to a man in Cumberland, and the former said, 'Just see the difference between us: the winner went home, and on the strength of his success got drunk for a fortnight, and his business is nearly ruined ; but I went home determined to succeed, and be at the top of the tree, and I now have over 200 men at work, and my churns and other dairy appliances go all over the world.' Since that Oxford meeting the 'Laval' cream separator has been invented and perfected, and has created almost a revolution in dairy work.

I was one of the judges at that terrible meeting at Kilburn. Nothing could exceed the misery everyone had to undergo in that ' Serbonian bog' ; it was impossible to walk a yard without a plank or wattled hurdle to put the feet on, and it rained the whole time. I was there eight days before the show opened, to decide on the merits of the railway waggons for the carriage of dead meat through the country. My fellow judges and I packed the competing vans with beef, mutton, veal, and pork, with hares, rabbits, fowls, ducks and geese, and sent them off to Holyhead, and back. On their return we opened them to see how the meat had stood the journey of 500 miles in the hot month of July. This competition was for a prize of 100*l*. offered by the Lord Mayor and Corporation of the City of London, and was considered of the greatest importance for the public ; and after a severe test the prize was given to the 'Glamorganshire Waggon Company,' greatly to the discomfiture of our Yankee friends, who had made sure of winning the coveted honour. It was, however, a useless prize, as

ENSILAGE AND SIR JOHN ASTLEY 135

the van was never afterwards used. All the competing waggons were laden on the top, sides, and ends with ice, and the cost of the material and the weight of the ice prevented it ever being in general use. Nor was it of any practical value, as meat is daily sent from Aberdeen, in properly prepared ordinary meat vans, in excellent order; but when thousands of miles have to be traversed, as they are in America and Canada, and from Lemberg, Vienna, &c., to Paris, it is of great consequence to have some means by which dead meat can be safely conveyed such long distances. At this meeting at Kilburn I had also to judge the foreign cattle, with Baron de Felcourt, a polite and able Frenchman. There were not many foreign cattle there, and although tolerably good animals, far below the magnificent specimens of our country.

My last appointment by the Royal was about four years ago, when, in connection with five others, I was to decide on the Silos, and manufacture of Ensilage. This was one of the most agreeable and interesting of all the subjects on which I have been employed. I travelled 4,500 miles, all over England and Wales, and had more opportunities of seeing the farming of my native country than I ever had before. Our reports have been published by the society, and are of great value. There was one point we established, viz. that it was not necessary to build an expensive silo at all, but that a stack of ensilage, well pressed down, answered every purpose.

One of the most agreeable of the places we visited, during our tour of inspection, was that of Sir John

Astley's, near Brigg, in Lincolnshire. The genial and popular baronet had invited most of his tenantry and many of his friends to meet us at a handsome luncheon, and then to proceed and open the silo. I should have stated in the outset that, for the purpose of our tour, the country was divided into three parts. The northern consisted of all the kingdom north and north-west of Warwick—this was the portion given to me and my colleague; the eastern and south-eastern, reaching from Norwich to Brighton and Dover; and the west and south-western, with a part of South Wales, the remainder. It so happened that when visiting Sir John Astley's my brother judge, Mr. George Baker, was prevented attending that day, and the brunt of the visit devolved upon me. The silo was opened and the silage proved excellent. When the hay or grass was cut it had been raining hard daily, and when the silo was being filled it rained in torrents, till the men, having been wetted through, could go on no longer, and the water ran out of the bottoms of the carts and waggons; and yet the ensilage was sweet, and most excellent for the cattle, who devoured it ravenously. It had been a dry spring, and the fly had been very prevalent, and the turnip and root crop was a great failure; but it showed that, by the judicious making of ensilage, a large quantity of valuable food could be obtained for winter use by this process. I showed my audience that the cost of a crop of tares, or other succulent food, when converted into ensilage, did not amount to more than 4*l.* per acre, whereas a root crop would have cost at least 10*l.* or 12*l.* I came home with one firm conviction, that wherever I went there was a universal belief that under present circumstances nothing but ruin must be the lot of the arable farmer. By the terms of our directions from the society, one of each department of the country had to traverse all the other portions before the final award was made. The prize of one hundred guineas went to a gentleman in Herefordshire.

I also was judge at Altona for the Schleswig-Holstein show, and was at Hamburg for more than a week, and enjoyed my visit to that beautiful city. I should have enjoyed it much more if I had not been *done* out of all recompense for my services, not to mention even my railway and hotel expenses. It cost me more than 30*l*., and although I was continually promised the money, I never had a farthing. My advice is, to any solicitations to judge abroad, never to go until you have the cash down before starting. I have also judged in the poultry department at Amsterdam, and four years ago I was president of the jury at the International Agricultural Exhibition at Brussels, at all of which places nothing could exceed the kindness and attention given to the representatives of England. I have elsewhere spoken of my judging at Vienna; and may say that a judge's position is not a very enviable one, as he has many people to please, and is almost sure to be roundly abused by disappointed exhibitors. In the practice of his vocation he sees many things that the public do not see, and although, in addition to my Royal and foreign experiences, I have adjudicated at Harrogate, Norwich, Halsted, Llanidloes, Hereford, Evesham, Worcester, Launceston, Plymouth, Rye in

Sussex, Bicester, Buckingham, Hatfield, Watford, and many other places, I generally get off without much personal disfavour, although probably mistakes are often made. *A propos* of judging, I remember an excellent story of my old friend, the late Henry Corbet, who was a famous judge of horses. He was judging in the hunter and hack classes at Peterborough, and there was a very numerous entry. The judges kept sending one horse after another out of the ring, till at last only three were left in. After grave consideration two more were sent out, and the prize given to the remaining horse. On Corbet coming from the ring a friend said, 'Corbet, do you see what you have done? You have given the prize to a *lame 'un*.' 'Yes,' said Corbet, 'we know that, but he's not half so lame as the other two!'

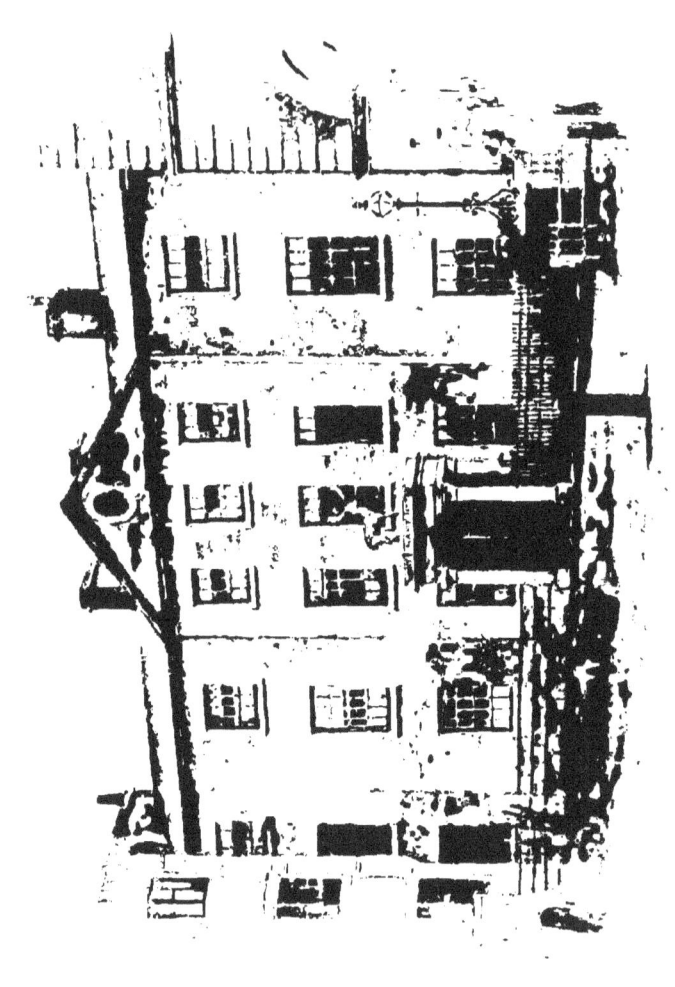

CHAPTER XIII

Steam cultivation—Advance in agricultural pursuits—Costume—Story of a smock frock—Poultry farming—Cochins, &c.—Statistics of poultry-keeping—The rinderpest—Old Fuchsia and her progeny—Immense prices—The bull Earl of Darlington built up in a faggot pile—John Clayden of Littlebury—and Home Cattle Defence Association—Quotation of Virgil and rinderpest—Marshal MacMahon—M. Tisserand de Bort at Paris Exhibition—Fashions at the dinner-table.

MANY alterations in the practice of agriculture have taken place during the last fifty years; and one of the most important is that of steam cultivation and the general introduction of steam for almost all farming operations. I read a paper upon two occasions at the Farmers' Club on the application of steam to agriculture, and about twenty-five years ago it was considered the great panacea for all the troubles of the farmer; but it is wonderful how steam cultivation in England has suddenly seemed to collapse. I have never been able to discover quite why it has been given up. In my own case I am willing to allow that, although I had my own set of tackle, I relinquished it after seven years' use, as I found I grew more weeds, and my wheat was apt to fall before harvest from being what is called 'weak-kneed,' probably the soil being rather too loose to hold it up. But where steam has been so beneficial to agriculture is in the establishment of railways, the influence of which has wonderfully altered the whole system of cultivation in many districts; and it gave to the farmer opportunities of getting a better market for his produce, and created in him a feeling of a desire to advance scientifically as well as personally, and in consequence his family was better educated, his household was more refined, and even his costume and personal appearance improved. The smock frock was abolished, and the broadcloth clothed the outer man. I remember a story, told me by a facetious farmer, of a circumstance that happened in the year 1814. After the Allies had entered Paris, and Napoleon had been banished to Elba, peace had been proclaimed, and the allied sovereigns came to England; amongst other places which they visited was Ashridge, near Great Berkhamstead, the seat of the Earl of Bridgwater. The Earl was desirous of showing them the class of men who tilled the soil, and who were the tenant farmers of England. So he invited his leading tenants to meet the allied sovereigns at dinner, but some of them were in the habit of wearing the old white smock frock, which was thought derogatory by the bulk of the tenants. This garment was very elaborately stitched—over the shoulders and down to the waist—and was a useful garment, as it was cool in summer and very warm in winter. The agent of the estate thought it was scarcely dignified enough to meet these great men with this countrified apparel, and the order went forth that all those who came to the dinner should discard the smock, and appear in broadcloth. Great was the dismay of many of them, but none was sadder than old Master Ezra Mullens, of Eddlesborough, who was one

A GRAND DINNER AND THE SMOCK FROCK 143

of the oldest and most respected of the tenants on the estate, and he very reluctantly consulted the village Poole, who at last completed a coat of broadcloth, which entirely encased the wearer. To elucidate the point of the story, my readers should understand that when the smock is worn at meal times, as it stretches across the knees, a sort of bag is formed, and at the termination of the meal the crumbs, and small portions of cheese, &c. collected there, are caught up in the hand, and forthwith thrown into the mouth. The important day arrived, and the place of honour, near the top of the table, was assigned to Master Ezra, and the Earl called him up and put him there, as the oldest tenant on the estate. The old man pushed his chair far away from the table, and leaned well forward, and ate a hearty meal. When he thought all was finished, a plate containing half a partridge, with bread sauce and fried crumbs, was put before him, and when in the act of dividing the leg of the bird, the plate was overbalanced, and down it fell between his legs, breaking the plate, and landing the contents on the floor. Great was the consternation of the guests, but Ezra turned piteously to his host and said, ' *There, my lord, dang this 'ere coat; if I'd ha' had on my smock I should a' cotched it all.*'

The public are every now and then regaled in the daily and weekly press with dissertations on the great neglect of the cultivation and rearing of poultry, and assert that the great panacea for farming is *going in* largely for poultry farming. I don't think anyone has a greater right to speak on this subject than myself, and I think it is ridiculous that farmers in general should be expected to do as I have done or meet with the same success, as mine was a collection of pure exhibition poultry, and the prices obtained were quite fancy. Shortly after taking my farm, being always fond of rearing fowls, I bought some fine specimens from a gentleman who had been very successful in the show-yard, and in the spring I bought a sitting of white Cochin eggs, for which I gave Mr. Baily, in Mount Street, two guineas. From these I reared six chickens, two cockerels and four pullets. I entered a trio, as was then the custom, at Anerley, which was the precursor of the present Crystal Palace shows, and won with them the special Cochin cup of ten guineas, and sold them to Sir Joseph Paxton for the same sum. I sent the other three chickens rather later in the season to Worcester, and won the ten-guinea cup there, and sold them at the same price, so that I made 42*l.* out of this venture. I mention this as a specimen of what can be done with care and good management. This started me on my hobby, and when I was in what is called full swing with my poultry, I generally had, on my farm of about 250 acres, a thousand head, consisting of Dorkings two sorts, Bramahs two sorts, Cochins three sorts, Game three sorts, Leghorns two sorts, Spanish, Minorcas, Plymouth Rocks, Houdans, Crève-cœur, Andalusians, Silkies, Indian game, as also varieties of Water-fowl, Aylesbury, Pekin, Rouen, East Indian and Cayuga ducks, besides White Embden and Toulouse geese, and American turkeys. For many years I sold about 400 sittings of eggs at 15*s.* per sitting, gained about 160*l.* in prizes, and the sale of the birds—scarcely ever under a guinea each, with eggs and poultry for my household use—averaged about 1,200*l*., and the profit made was about 300*l*. per annum. I admit this is exceptional, and I doubt if any other person could show such a result. It became an important branch of my business, and I have sent eggs and birds to all parts of the world—America, Canada, New Zealand, Australia, Cape of Good Hope, Brazil, West Indies, Russia, Germany, Austria, Belgium, Holland, and even to France, where I successfully competed with this well-known and justly esteemed poultry country, and won the gold medal at their great international show in Paris in 1878, and also won the gold medal for fowls, and the same for water-fowl at the great show at Amsterdam a few years later. I hope I may be pardoned for blowing my own trumpet on this subject, but I wished to show my readers that we can equal, if not surpass, our Continental neighbours in this industry. As a rule I think there is no department on a farm more grossly neglected than the poultry-yard; and if farmers who think this branch of their business beneath their notice will bear in mind that in 1892 England imported 1,200,000,000 eggs and paid more than 583,430*l*. for dead poultry, it will open their eyes to the value of poultry rearing. In addition to this there is the great value of the denizens of the poultry-yard in the destruction of grubs, insects and their larvæ, slugs and numberless pests, the eggs of which are deposited in manure, and carted away upon the land to destroy the fruits of the farmer's labour annually.

When the rinderpest, or real cattle plague, broke out in England, I had a very valuable herd of short-horns.

This terrible scourge took place in the years 1865-6, and many curious events happened in connection with it. I had seen in one of the agricultural papers an advertisement of three Bell-Bates females for sale, mother, daughter, and I believe granddaughter, belonging to Captain Blathwayt. I wrote to him for price, and he asked 150 guineas for the three. After several letters I agreed to give him 120 guineas for them without seeing them, only going by their exceptionally good pedigrees. One was Old Fuchsia, and the others were called 'Fidgets.' I gave directions for them to be sent by railway from near Clifton, but on that very day came out the Orders in Council to prohibit the transit of all cattle throughout the country, on account of the rinderpest, and the bargain was thus at an end. At Captain Blathwayt's sale, a few years afterwards, Old Fuchsia stood in his park in all her grandeur, over sixteen years of age, one of the finest cows ever seen, and was retained by her owner, whilst her descendants, two of which I had agreed to buy at 40 guineas each, made 700 and 500 guineas, and two others of the same blood brought 350 and 300 guineas each. If I had had the good fortune to have completed my bargain, which a delay of a few hours in the appearance of the order would have enabled me to do, I should have made several thousand pounds, as these cows had been very prolific, and the Bates blood had risen enormously in value during the past few years. Since that time I have had the pleasure of attending at Lord Dunmore's and Lord Bective's sales, and have seen thousands of pounds bid for cows and bulls, where but a few years previously

OUTBREAK IN ENGLAND OF THE RINDERPEST 147

400*l.* or 500*l.* would have been considered enormous. Now whilst I am writing prices have receded to their old level, and even much lower, but I believe that when trade revives, and the great manufacturing and trading firms want an outlet for their superabundant capital, the fashion for this exciting pursuit, and the pleasure of rearing this beautiful tribe of cattle, will again be revived, but never again shall we see the almost fabulous prices of old. No account of short-horn breeding would be complete without a notice of the terrible outbreak, unknown in England until the years 1865-6, of the rinderpest, which had been often described by travellers in Eastern Russia. It is impossible to describe the terror which this disease caused amongst all classes, and after much discussion and consultation with medical men and veterinary professors, and after several remedies had been tried without success, the ministry of the day came to the conclusion that there was no way of stopping the plague except by slaughtering every animal attacked, and those which had been in contact with them. I trust that for many years to come this dire disease may not reappear in this country, but it may nevertheless be of some interest to record its effect on the poor creatures who suffered. After the commencement of the attack, which produces shivering and inflammation of the mucous membranes, the lungs become inflamed and a painful cough ensues, which rapidly increases; the hair becomes erect, cutaneous eruptions break out, with inability to move, simulating paralysis; emaciation is very rapid. The poor animal stands with its legs drawn together under the body, exhaustion of the vital forces follows, and failure of the heart's action, and asphyxia ends the life of the wretched creature, for whom after it is once attacked there is little or no hope. My neighbourhood had been most seriously affected, and as it was a great dairy district, and within forty miles of London, it made a centre peculiarly sensitive. I was in great fear about my valuable herd of short-horns, but by complete isolation of my cattle, and fumigation of my herdsmen's clothes and persons, and washing all the animals daily with a slight solution of carbolic acid, in my case 'the plague was stayed.'

I cannot refrain from telling an amusing story to show how in some cases the law was evaded. An old-fashioned dairyman named Kingsley, living about six miles from me, bought a good bull at Lord Penrhyn's sale, called Earl of Darlington, of which he was not only very proud but very fond. The disease had settled on his farm, and the whole of his cattle were ordered to be slaughtered and buried. He was resolved to save his favourite bull, and one morning the police and the official butcher commenced operations and were nearly two days completing their work. When they had finished the cows and calves, they asked for the famous bull, but he could not be found anywhere. It was thought that he had strayed, and after a diligent search they gave up the job. The fact was, Master Kingsley *had built him up in a faggot pile*, the centre being left hollow. A large tub was placed for water, and at night, from the top the faggots were removed, buckets of water were poured down, hay and roots lowered, and the faggots again replaced. Thus the bull was saved after being incarcerated some weeks, when he was released safe and sound, and did good service in the new herd for some years afterwards. At last the Government became alive to the havoc and destruction to which the live stock of the kingdom was being subjected, and closed all the markets and fairs throughout the country. The late Mr. John Clayden of Littlebury, near Saffron Walden, one of the most noted farmers in England, became chairman of the 'Home Cattle Defence Association,' whilst I was vice-chairman, and we were chiefly instrumental in establishing the principle, for many years adhered to, of slaughtering all cattle at the ports of debarkation. It appears that this terrible scourge was for the first time introduced into England in the early part of the last century, and the disease must have been known to the Romans, as I remember, in the third Georgic of Virgil, the following quotation, evidently alluding to the rinderpest:

> It tristis arator
> Mærentem abjungens fraternâ morte juvencum.

The losses caused by the rinderpest in Great Britain were computed to amount from these outbreaks to quite ten million pounds sterling!

The announcement in 'The Times' of this morning (October 18, 1893) of the death of the celebrated French Marshal MacMahon, who was the youngest but one of seventeen children, and of pure Irish descent, brings to my recollection that I once had the honour of a pleasing introduction to and an interview with him when I had charge of the cattle, poultry, and other live stock at the

Paris Exhibition, 1878. The Exhibition was held in the Place des Invalides, and a few days before the close, M. Tisserand de Bort, the Minister of Agriculture, held a great reception at his official residence of the jury and exhibitors of agricultural live stock, and the staff of the Exhibition with Sir Philip Cunliffe-Owen. The reception was held in the splendid *salons* of the official residence of the minister, and the numerous company were regaled with fine French wines and handsome refreshments, and the courteous minister moved about amongst his guests, conversing on agricultural subjects, with which he seemed to be quite *au fait*, in fairly good English, speaking in high terms of the wonderful show made by the English exhibitors, and expressing his opinion that it could not fail to exercise a great influence on the future of the agriculture of France. He admired particularly the beauty of the short-horn cattle, and sheep, especially the Southdowns and Shropshires, which he thought were unrivalled. We had a long discussion together on the merits of the Charolais, Flamande, and other French breeds, but we agreed that the former, beautiful as they were, could not for a moment be compared to the polled Angus for flesh production ; nor could their best milkers bear a comparison for profitable use with our short-horns, as they were almost useless for beef after they had ceased milking ; yet the Flamande, and some others, were large-framed fine animals, and gave a great quantity of rich, good milk. He asked me to meet him the next day, and go round the show with him. After our meeting we observed a commotion round the entrance, and it was announced that the President of the Republic,

Marshal MacMahon, had arrived. Monsieur hurried me on, and said he wished to introduce me to the President. I had observed that he had come in a very unostentatious manner, in a plain chariot, with a pair of horses, without any military escort, and on his alighting from his carriage I saw a very military, nice-looking gentleman step out, in plain morning suit, frock-coat, closely buttoned, and a tall hat, and salute the few persons who had come around him. When M. Tisserand de Bort introduced me, and said I had brought over and was superintending the English cattle and poultry, the President said he wished to see the Queen's cattle. I took him to Her Majesty's short-horns, and explained their chief points, and then to the Marquis of Exeter's noted bull Telemachus, and from there to the Duke of Buckingham's long-horns, with which he expressed much astonishment. He was also pleased with Mr. Duncan's Highlanders, with their ruddy shaggy hides and widespreading horns, and when I showed him Mr. M'Combie's beautiful black polled Angus, the group which had obtained the premium and the special prize of fine Sèvres China as the best cattle in the exhibition, he admired them greatly. I then hurriedly showed him some of the sheep classes, especially the four-horned Dorsets. Before leaving he asked me if I had exhibited anything, and on learning that I had he expressed a desire to see them. Accordingly I took him to my short-horn heifer, Graffin Foggathorpe, who had an Honourable Mention, with which animal he was much pleased. He then thanked me for my attention, and went on to the main Exhibition. Altogether it was a very agreeable hour, and I have always considered it a great honour to have been introduced to so distinguished a soldier and so prominent a man as the President of the French Republic, and the incident reminded me strongly of my introduction to the Emperor Franz Joseph, at the Vienna Exhibition a few years before.

The fashion prevalent in the present century, until about thirty years since, of remaining at the dinner-table long after the repast had concluded has completely changed. There were certainly many advantages in this genial old custom. The dinner was rather more substantial than at present, if not so varied; the practice of challenging or taking wine with each other and pledging healths during dinner was usually observed, which to us of the present day seems somewhat foolish, but many an old family feud or personal quarrel was smoothed over by this plan; even the ladies were expected to respond, and in each case her next-door neighbour, or the butler, partly filled her glass, and with a benign bow to the challenger she sipped the hock, sherry, or bucellas, and then waited for the next summons. The host would, during dinner, challenge all his guests together to a glass of wine, and then, after much smiling and joking, would deliberately bow to those on each side of the board, and give a special recognition of love to his better half, who presided at the other end of the table. The now almost universal habit of drinking champagne at a dinner party would have made the old plan almost impossible, as it necessitates the wine being handed round by the servants, and not put on the table, as was done with the still wines then in vogue. When dinner was over, the table-cloth was removed, and the brightly polished oak or mahogany was exposed, reflecting the silver candlesticks and candelabra, and perhaps a centre-piece with fruits piled up on it. The dessert was placed on the shining table, and the silver knives, forks, and spoons, and china plates placed before each guest; and the rare old port was passed round, not handed and poured out as at present in one single glass, and oftentimes only three parts filled. Conversation became general, and about half an hour afterwards, the dessert having been finished, the hostess rose after a significant look round, and the ladies in a procession left the room, the gentlemen rising and bowing them out. Then the gentlemen gathered round the host, and the wine was attacked with due vigour. It was then that stories were told, the events of the day, if it had been a hunting or a shooting party, were discussed, and rarely if ever was smoking permitted, as it would utterly destroy the true flavour and character of the wines. With the general run of stories those relating to port and other wines were most popular, and amongst many that I have heard none to me seemed of greater interest than that which I am going to relate. The Bucks volunteers, of which regiment I was Quartermaster, were encamped in Claydon Park, the residence of my revered friend Sir Harry Verney. He asked me to go over his stock of wine in the vaults under the mansion, as there were certain bins of wine rather deficient in character, and some were undrinkable from their great age. He came down into the cellars with me and I carefully sampled the contents. I discovered a bin of wine which completely baffled my judgment. Sir Harry said none of the family would drink it, as it had become decayed. I minutely examined it; it was in curious old-fashioned bottles, was of a really beautiful colour, a light ruby, *not tawny*, and I pronounced it perfectly sound because there was no acetous fermentation. There was, however, scarcely any rich flavour, and at last I discovered in the bottom of some of the bottles large flakes of crust, which I found had slipped off the sides, and were then floating in the wine, but they did not discolour or foul it; on again tasting it I felt sure it was port, evidently of great age. Sir Harry then fetched an old wine book of his father's, and the mystery was solved. His father, General Calvert (Sir Harry having taken the name of Verney on succeeding to the Claydon property), was Quartermaster-general to the Duke of Wellington throughout the Peninsular War. When the British army was safely encamped and protected in the masterly lines constructed by the great Duke at Torres Vedras, in or about 1809, Mr. Sandeman, the head of the great wine house at Oporto, was a frequent guest at the duke's dinner-table, and the conversation once turned upon fine and noted vintages. Mr. Sandeman said he thought the vintage of 1797 was the finest port wine ever known, and that vintage was as much talked of then as the 1834, '47, or '51 vintages are talked of now. General Calvert, as a great favour, requested him to send two pipes of this celebrated wine to England. Mr. Sandeman did so, and the general made a present of one to the Duke of York, at that time commander-in-chief of the army; and the other he had bottled for himself, and this was the remains of that very wine. Sir Harry wished to get rid of it, and I agreed to exchange as many dozens of the finest 1873, which I had lately shipped from Martinez and Gassiot, as there were dozens of the 1797. He was well pleased with the bargain, and I found there were nineteen dozens of it. When I got it home into my vaults, I drew out six dozen from each of two pipes of 1873, and blended the same amount of the last century wine, and bottled it in 1876, and in three years' time it turned out some of the finest wine I ever tasted. I sold six dozen of the original port to Messrs. Spiers & Pond through their well-known buyer Mr. William Hudson, at a moderate price, and the following Christmas, at the dinner of the Farmers' Club, at the Criterion, I observed in the special wine list, 'Duke of York's port,' vintage 1797, price 2*l*. per bottle. I heard that at this well-known establishment this wine was often called for, and that it is much appreciated. I have heard many port wine stories, but I think this beats the record. I have one or two bottles in my present cellars, and hope to live to open one at the hundredth anniversary of the vintage. General Calvert became the duke's adjutant-general at Waterloo, and was a very distinguished and able officer. This wine when I tasted it was therefore eighty years old, and shows how well a really grand wine will keep sound. *A propos* of port wine, I had at one time a young French gentleman, a farm pupil, residing with me, who was very fond of port, and I once remarked that it was 'the king of all wines.' ' No, sir,' he said, '*it is the emperor*,' and my own opinion is, that there is no wine so grand and truly great as a fine vintage port, bottled young— say after three or four years in the wood—and drunk from twelve to fifteen years afterwards.

CHAPTER XIV

Mr. Robert Ceely — Vaccination Experiments — The Night-flowering Cereus — The Agricultural Labourer — His Varied Occupations — His Wages — Pleasures of Agricultural Life — The Effect of Railways on Agriculture.

SOME years ago a very serious outbreak of smallpox occurred in England, and all the medical profession were agitated about it. Mr. Robert Ceely, an eminent medical practitioner, who lived next door to my home, had made the subject of vaccination his especial study. The main point of his experiments was to verify Dr. Jenner's theory that the product of vaccination was modified small-pox, and that the pus from a small-pox pustule, when made to pass through the cow, would become so diluted as to be practically harmless. Mr. Ceely therefore tried numberless experiments on various animals, and kept them in some buildings and a paddock adjoining our gardens and pleasure grounds, and I had many opportunities of watching the progress of his investigations. He had goats, heifers, young colts, sheep, a donkey, and a monkey on which to try his hand, and after many weeks of constant attention in doing what Jenner and many others, especially the Germans, had failed to do, he obtained fine pustules on the tender parts of the skin of two heifers ; he had them most carefully copied by a competent artist, as photography was then only in its infancy, and when these were compared with many small-pox eruptions they were pronounced to be perfectly similar. His next step was to pass the lymph from the pustules of these heifers into the human subject, and thus produce the appearance of actual small-pox. At that time he had an old fellow named Brown, a sort of odd man in the garden, and on him he tried his first experiment, and I shall never forget Mr. Ceely coming in to see my father, and with great glee saying, ' By Jove! I am glad to tell you old Brown is so ill I found him lying helpless under the manger in the stable. I got him out and have put him to bed. It is the most splendid case I could have imagined.' The old chap got better in a few days, and it was found he had a magnificently inflamed arm, like a perfectly vaccinated limb ; and from him several children were operated upon, all of them with wonderful success, and the vaccine lymph was sent all over the kingdom, and thus enabled a new departure to be made of the vaccine matter, which was thought to have become much impaired from continuous use for more than sixty years. This experiment was much commented on at the time as having been the first proven case since Jenner's day. Mr. Ceely published his book on ' Variolæ Vaccinæ,' which is the text-book on this marvellous discovery, and proves Jenner's theory to be true, that vaccination was really modified small-pox. Old Brown soon got well, and continued his labours in the garden, and the tending of ' them there *weathergated* plants,' which he persisted in calling all *variegated* geraniums and other flowers of that class now so prevalent. A great joke was perpetrated by some young fellows, two of whom were medical students, after these experiments. They secured the donkey patient, and painted him with black and white stripes like a zebra, and placed him in an adjoining field to the experimental paddock during the night preceding the market day. The farmers and other country people were astonished to see, as they thought, a zebra quietly grazing in the field, and they were informed, much to their astonishment, that this was the effect of Mr. Ceely's experiment of vaccination, which had turned the donkey into a zebra.

Mr. Ceely had a remarkable mania for the cultivation of the cactus, and had nearly every variety of the prickly deformity for which this unsatisfactory plant is noted. But amongst them he succeeded in growing that remarkable and very beautiful variety, the night-flowering Cereus. When these were in bloom—which was not until the hour of nine or ten o'clock P.M.—he invited large parties of ladies to view them, and his greenhouses were filled till past midnight with visitors to see these really beautiful flowers, and on one occasion he had as many as thirty-six very large blooms expanded at one time. The peculiarity of this night-flowering plant is that it only blooms in perfection about midnight, and before sunrise it is utterly gone. On one occasion, when Mr. Ceely had been summoned to give evidence before a coroner's jury at an inquest on an old man in the village of Bishopstone, who had died suddenly, he left the place and went to an adjoining village about three miles away, before the verdict was given, to attend on a patient, and on his return he met one of the jurymen, who was an old-fashioned village farmer, and asked him how they had brought in the verdict. The sapient juryman replied, 'Oh, just as you said, Muster Ceely—"died o' the blessing o' God."' Mr. Ceely was appointed by the Government and acted for many years as one of the inspectors on the outbreak of small-pox, and was one of the Royal Commission on the cattle plague, or rinderpest, when this terrible scourge destroyed so many thousand head of cattle and ruined the prospects of numbers of farmers throughout the kingdom. He was a most eminent medical man and was called in consultation on many serious cases in the county. He died a few years since at the age of eighty-two, beloved by all who knew him. He was chiefly instrumental, with that benevolent baronet Sir Harry Verney—now in his ninety-third year—in founding that excellent institution, the Bucks General Infirmary, and his portrait now hangs in the board-room alongside that of Sir Harry.

A long and intimate connexion with farming, both at home and abroad, for upwards of fifty years, must be my apology for introducing my agricultural recollections to the public. Many changing phases of this most delightful and interesting occupation have taken place during that period, from great prosperity to absolute despair. I do not pretend to be a learned chemist, nor am I a noted mechanician, but I have been a manual worker in nearly every department, and have thoroughly enjoyed my labour. I have come to the conclusion that no occupation, to him who is called a working man, is so full of pleasure and variation. If Hodge is not in receipt of wages equal to the worker in the great towns, he has his labour in the fresh open air, and an ever-changing variety of occupation following the seasons. He has his fixed hours of coming and going, he has generally a good roomy cottage, certainly without many of the so-called modern improvements; a fairly productive garden, giving him a supply of vegetables for his family; often a stye for a pig, and out-house for wood, &c., in which he can keep a few fowls; and if he has a constant place in winter and summer, though his wages may seem small, they are regularly paid, and he has not much to complain of. His wages should not be calculated at only the ordinary rate at which he is paid, as he gets extra money at times. Thus, 14$s.$ per week for the ordinary labourer, and 16$s.$ per week for the Sunday men—carters, cowmen, and shepherds —represented only a portion of their earnings, as in hay and harvest 24$s.$ to 28$s.$ or 30$s.$ per week were often paid, and this brought up the average for my men, for the whole year, to 17$s.$ 9$d.$ per week; to this must be added beer at hay, harvest, threshing and other times. But the chief advantage to a country labourer, living in a rural village, is the cheapness of his house rent: often it is only a shilling a week for a cottage and a fairly good garden. One of my men complained to me that his rent had been raised from 1$s.$ 4$d.$ to 1$s.$ 6$d.$ per week; he had nearly a rood of garden, and some good bearing fruit trees. This is a great contrast to the condition of a London workman. I was in the train a short time since, returning to Hampton, and at Vauxhall a rather grimy-looking young man entered the carriage, and I found him a very sensible and intelligent fellow. The conversation turned upon house rent, and he told me that for one room and a small set off at Vauxhall he used to pay 5s. 6d. a week. He was an engine cleaner on the South Western line, and he had taken a cottage at Feltham, where he had a nice parlour, a good kitchen and two bedrooms, with a fair-sized garden, for which he paid 5s. a week, and the company allowed him to travel on the line for 1s. per week from and to his work; so it cost him 6d. a week extra to live in the fresh air. In addition to this he was able to grow nearly enough vegetables, except potatoes, for his family, and his wife and three children were now healthy and strong, whereas in Vauxhall they were generally ailing. I then told him my men had a better cottage at 1s. 6d.; he said he had 24s. per week, and he thought 14s. for my men was as good pay as 24s. to him, or at all events they were as well off. There was much philosophy in this, and I fully endorse his opinion. Yet there is much room for improvement in village cottage accommodation, and Lord Beaconsfield was quite right in saying that the chief considerations for a good cottage for the agricultural labourer were 'an oven, a tank, and a porch.' It is also the fashion to run Hodge down, and dilate on his inherent stupidity. This is not my opinion of him; as a rule he is quite equal in intellect to his brother in the manufacturing towns. His employment is ever-varying, scarcely two days alike, whilst the same constant drudge of men at the loom, and at other manufacturing employments, day after day, is without any variation. The luckier Hodge can contemplate the budding of the trees, the blossoms on the hedge banks, the springing up and gradual development of the corn crops, the flowering of the beans and peas, the sowing, hoeing, and setting out of the root crops, the mowing and carting of the hay and clover, the gathering in of the corn harvest, the threshing and making up of the grain for market, and the preparation of the land for the next year's crop. The shepherd has a continuous change of occupation : the lambing season, the folding and pasturing of the flock, the shearing of the sheep, the weaning of the lambs, the feeding of the wedders for market. So also the herdsman has variety of occupation : the parturition of the cows, spreading over the whole year—contrary to the shepherd's work, as all the ewes bring forth about the same time—the milking of the cows, the rearing of the calves, and the various occupations of field and dairy work, make a constant change for the exercise of his faculties. The great variety of the daily avocation of the agricultural labourer has a tendency to develop his thinking powers to a greater extent than is the case with his urban brother ; but his isolation in his country village, the few opportunities he has of exchanging his opinions with his fellow man, except in the village ale-house, tend to warp his mind, and to give him prejudices which are difficult to eradicate.

Yet his outdoor life is pleasing to the ploughman, with the smell of the newly turned-up soil and the breathing of the fresh air. The scent of the milking kine, and the smell even of the sheepfold, are agreeable to the senses ; and although his fare is coarse and ill-prepared, yet it is generally ample, and the feeling of independence, as he saunters by the hedgerows, is fed by this outdoor existence, and gives him that health and strength denied to the workman in manufacturing towns and great cities. To a certain extent these same feelings are engrafted into the minds and even the habits of his master, the tenant-farmer; and the thoughts and practices of the landlord and country gentleman are in the same way influenced as the humblest of the field-labourers. The introduction, however, of railways has caused a revolution in the minds of country people, as also in the routine of cropping and cultivating the land. I need but instance the remarkable increase in the milk consumption of London and other great towns. Had it not been for the advantage of quick transport afforded by the railways this enormous amount of milk could not have been carried, and let us hope that this development has afforded some palliation for the distress now prevailing in the agricultural districts. Yet in the great panacea proposed by the *would-be* advisers of the British farmer, viz. to lay down arable land into pasture, there is one thing these wiseacres have forgotten—*what is to be done for a water supply* for cattle in those waterless districts on the hill countries, where the larger portion of the arable land is to be found? What would the live stock do on the beech-clad Chilterns, and on the Berkshire, Wiltshire, and Hampshire downs? How would the cattle on the Cotswolds and the Mendips fare, or on some of the claylands of Essex? There have been over thirty thousand acres of land absorbed by railways and the approaches to stations, but the immense advantages to the community in general have fully compensated for the loss of cultivated land. Steam cultivation, a few years since, played a great part in the improvement of agriculture, but from one cause or another the system has been nearly abandoned. I had my own set of apparatus, which was worked by the ordinary labourers on my farm, except the steam-engine itself. I was watching one of these machines at work one day when a young man who was one of my carters was riding and steering the implement. The sun was setting like a ball of fire, and disappearing or dipping rapidly behind a hill in the near distance, when he turned round and said to his assistants, 'Look at the sun; they told me at school that the sun don't move, but I say it does, and I wish some of those fellows would come and see it. Ah! there it goes! Now it's out of sight and I know, and you know, as it does move.' All the scientific teaching of the National or the Board schools could not alter the fact as it appeared to them, and my young carter, after my attempts to explain the phenomenon to him, said, 'Ah, sir, don't try to deceive me. I see the sun go down, and so might you if you had been looking.'

CHAPTER XV

The Rothschild family—They settle in Bucks—Establishment of the staghounds—Opposition of Duke of Buckingham—Judæa—A romantic 'Varsity story—Inter-'Varsity steeplechases—Point to point 'chases—Ladies hunting—Empress of Austria.

IN my native county of Bucks the advent of the great family of the Rothschilds has had a marked effect on the life and habits of the people round about them, whether labourers, farmers, or gentlefolk, and their contact with country life has reacted on themselves, and has brought out the instincts of love of rural life and sports which otherwise would not have been found if their lives had wholly been spent in the walls of cities and in the counting-houses of great financial centres. I believe it was in or about the year 1847, when the late Baron Lionel Rothschild, with his brothers Nathaniel, Anthony, and Meyer, partially took up their residence amongst us. This is not the place to describe in detail the circumstances which have made this marvellous family so popular and powerful in our midst, and what I relate is entirely from memory, and from many interesting conversations which I had with the late Mr. James James, one of the leading solicitors in Aylesbury, and an old schoolfellow of mine. Mr. James was quite the

ESTABLISHMENT OF THE STAGHOUNDS 167

right-hand man of the Rothschilds, and had boldly given the advice that if they wished to make themselves a power in the neighbourhood, as also in the State, they should concentrate their capital in or about one spot, and not buy an estate here and another there. He pointed out that the Vale of Aylesbury had many advantages from its contiguity to London, its rich, good land, its many fine sites for residences, and also from the fact that the country was held in small properties, which could probably be bought at a reasonable rate, and eventually this excellent advice was followed. One of the first things the Rothschilds did was to take over a pack of harriers kept by Mr. Adamson at Hastoe, near Tring, and about seven miles from Aylesbury; there were small kennels and moderate accommodation for horses and deer; and they commenced stag-hunting in 1847. Shortly after the neighbourhood was startled at the announcement that Baron Meyer had bought the Mentmore estate, for which I believe he gave something like 95,000*l*., and soon afterwards an old-fashioned farm-house was converted into a hunting-box, and, when kennels were built and accommodation made for the horses and men, the hunting establishment was brought there. Just at this time the country was agitated by Sir Robert Peel's abolition of the Corn Laws, and he alienated most of his Tory supporters from him. Bucks was torn to pieces by the discussions which ensued between the two parties. The Rothschilds were free traders, and therefore in favour of the abolition, while many of the farmers, believing the repeal would be ruinous to them, became very inimical to the hounds hunting over their land, and the Duke of Buckingham was not loth to make political capital out of this discontent, and prepared a notice to warn the Barons off the land, and obtained the signatures of all his tenants and a great number of their friends, with several of the local squires, to carry the notice into effect. This was a serious blow to the Rothschilds, as a large portion of the vale of Aylesbury,

THE BARON'S HOUNDS AT MENTMORE

including all the best grass country, would be alienated from them. My father, who had a farm at Broughton, situated between Aylesbury and Tring, although a staunch Tory, felt very indignant at the tyrannical conduct of the duke. He thought the Rothschilds had been shamefully treated, and got up a counterblast, and wrote to Baron Lionel inviting him to his farmhouse to breakfast, and to turn out the stag in the best field on his farm. The Baron readily accepted the invitation, and most of the independent gentry and farmers of the district were pleased at my father's pluck, and came in large numbers to the breakfast and the meet. The Barons Rothschild were delighted at the spirit shown, and for a time forebore to meet on or near the Duke's estates. This was the prelude to the well-known hospitality shown for many years afterwards at every farmhouse at which the hounds met.

The Broughton breakfast was simple, substantial farmhouse fare, fortified with orange and cherry brandy, good ale, and port and sherry, but by degrees this mild hospitality developed into a champagne breakfast, with every modern detail of expense; until the present Lord Rothschild, with that good sense which always characterises him, being determined to put down this hospitable rivalry, and knowing what the altered circumstances of the farmers had become, now advertises the meets at certain cross-roads or villages, instead of the farmhouses as formerly. I mention this circumstance to show what difficulties beset these energetic gentlemen at the outset of their hunting career. A year or two after the purchase of the Mentmore property, the Baron Meyer resolved to build a mansion worthy of his name, and Sir Joseph Paxton was consulted as to the site. I remember riding over with Mr. James to see the spot selected, and the designing of the building was placed in the hands of the architect, Mr. Stokes, a son-in-law of Sir Joseph, and the splendid mansion of Mentmore Towers was soon after completed. Just about that time the terrible crash of the Duke of Buckingham occurred, and nearly all his properties came to the hammer; some of these were purchased by the Rothschilds, and most of them passed into private hands, but they succeeded in buying them afterwards. I need but mention Aston Clinton, which in my youth was inhabited by Lord Lake, and afterwards belonged to Mr. Chapman, who was a banker in Aylesbury; it was purchased by the late Sir Anthony de Rothschild, to carry out his love of farming and country life. He altered and added largely to the house, and made it an unpretentious but charming residence. He laid out an extensive park, and built large farm premises, where he established a herd of short-horn cattle, and greatly improved the agriculture of the district. Lady de Rothschild now lives there with her daughter, the wife of Lord Battersea, who was formerly Mr. Cyril Flower. About this time the death of Sir John Dashwood, with his misfortunes, brought the Halton estate into the market, and that was purchased by Baron Lionel, and lately Mr. Alfred de Rothschild, his son, has built a lovely mansion on the side of the Chiltern Hills, commanding splendid views. The house is not too large, and is replete with every elegance and luxury. Cubitt, the architect and builder, I am told, had *carte blanche* to make the house perfect. The furniture and pictures, with the fittings, are magnificent. Some short time afterwards Miss Alice, the sister of Baron Ferdinand de Rothschild, bought the Eythorpe estate for 180,000*l*. This was once the property of the Earl of Chesterfield, and was sold to the Marquis d'Harcourt, who had purchased it a few years before, at the break up of the splendid estates when the Aston Abbotts, the Wing, the Wingrave, the Aston Clinton, Hogston, and other fine properties in Bucks were obliged to be sold. Miss Alice has laid out the site of the old mansion, which was pulled down in 1812, and from which the street front of the White Hart was built, with much taste, and has built a small residence, called a Water Pavilion, of great beauty, by the side of the river Thame, and the farmhouses and cottages have been erected from lovely designs by Mr. Devey. Then the Wing property was obtained, and a delightful hunting-box, with stabling, kennels, deer paddocks, and every necessary appliance was erected, and is now occupied by Mr. and Mrs. Leopold de Rothschild. Then the Waddesdon and Wichendon estates were purchased by Baron Ferdinand from the late Duke of Marlborough for about 240,000*l*., and the timber at a valuation in addition. There was no residence for an owner upon it, but Baron Ferdinand, who is a member of the Vienna family, has erected one of the grandest houses in England, and, for a private residence, scarcely to be matched in Europe; it is placed on the summit of Lodge Hill, overlooking the village of Waddesdon, and is about seven miles from Aylesbury. It is in the French style of architecture, designed by a Frenchman, but is scarcely in keeping with the English scenery surrounding it. The house is an immense size, and I have been told it will accommodate more than a hundred guests.

To give my readers some idea of the expensive manner in which the ornamental grounds have been laid out, I may mention that a great many oak and elm trees of a century old have been removed from the valley, and drawn up, and replanted on the hill, taking sixteen powerful horses to move them. I have seen large specimens of evergreens pass through Aylesbury, drawn on a heavy framework by twelve or more horses, and brought the whole way from Kent! I rode over with Mr. James to see the mansion when it was not more than three feet out of the ground, and he told me that to take off the top of the hill, to prepare it for the building and to make the roads up to it, cost 55,000*l.*, and the first contract for the shell of the house was 87,000*l.* The water supply has been brought from the works of the 'Chiltern Hills' Water Company, at the cost of many thousands of pounds, and supplies the various farms through which it passes. As the water comes from a high elevation and is sixteen miles from its source, it enables handsome fountains to play in the grounds, and provides the mansion with beautifully pure water. It is really a wonderful place, and when my brother visited it about two years ago, to advise the Baron about his dairy, he expressed himself astonished at the magnificence that he saw both in and outside the house. The Baron said, 'Yes, it ought to be a good property, for it has cost me over two millions of money.' Well enough may the Prince of Wales and other friends be often visitors to so fine a place; Her Majesty the Queen and the Shah of Persia have visited Waddesdon Manor, and have expressed their admiration at the mansion and the grounds, and the matchless landscape stretched around it, the whole vale of Aylesbury with nearly thirty miles of luxurious, well-cultivated land being visible.

FRED COX AND LORD ROTHSCHILD'S HOUNDS AT TRING PARK

Whilst all these vast undertakings were going on, the present Lord Rothschild—the eldest son of Baron Lionel, and long known as Sir Nathaniel, he having succeeded to the baronetcy of Sir Anthony, had bought of the Kaye trustees the Tring estate, mostly in Herts but only seven miles from Aylesbury, for which I think he gave 240,000*l.*, exclusive of timber. He has added largely to the beautiful mansion, once tenanted by Nell Gwynne, and made very extensive improvements, and, with its lovely deer-park, partly tenanted at the present time by the kangaroo, the emu, and other specimens of beast and bird life, tended and fostered by his eldest son, the Hon. Walter Rothschild, who has become a distinguished naturalist, well may the district be called 'Judæa'! Little could it have been imagined at the time my father gave the simple farmhouse hunt breakfast, as a protest against the unjustifiable conduct of the Duke of Buckingham, that such misfortunes would assail this historic family, or that whilst I am writing this the head of so distinguished a house as Rothschild would be Lord Lieutenant of the great historic county of Bucks, or when they had no residence in the neighbourhood there would now be seven important mansions within eight miles of Aylesbury inhabited by the Rothschild family: Mentmore, Lord Rosebery; Tring, Lord Rothschild; Aston Clinton, Lady Anthony; Halton, Mr. Alfred; Wing, Mr. Leopold; Eythorpe, Miss Alice; and Waddesdon, Baron Ferdinand de Rothschild; and that there would now be three peerages connected with the family: Earl Rosebery, who married Miss Hannah, Baron Meyer's only child; Lord Battersea, who married Sir Anthony's eldest daughter; and the last creation, Lord Rothschild, which indeed is a fit commentary on my remarks on country and agricultural life.

Somewhere about the year 1860 one of the most popular undergraduates in the University of Oxford was X. Y. (I forbear mentioning his name), and his story was a curious one. It was told me by himself a few years afterwards, and is such a perfect romance and so sad a story that I am tempted to record it. He was a really good fellow, fairly clever, young, handsome, and was in with all the best of the fast sets in the 'Varsity. My intimacy with him commenced with his visits to our aristocratic steeplechases, where he was always to be found. I don't think he performed as a gentleman jock over that celebrated course, but he generally entered a horse in the undergraduates' race. It was well known that he had but a limited allowance, and suddenly a collapse occurred, and he was obliged to leave his college. Shortly afterwards he was foolish enough to form a *liaison* with a lady of questionable character in London, and then privately married her. On his father hearing of it he was justly irritated, and found the means to send him to Canada, where he and his wife arrived with excellent letters of introduction. After a short time his agreeable and gentlemanlike manners succeeded in getting him an appointment as secretary to one of the ecclesiastical societies, and the bishop (I think of Toronto) took him by the hand and gave him his patronage. His wife was extremely handsome, and a presentable, well-educated woman, and she behaved with perfect manners and got the *entrée* into the best society.

He seemed to have fallen on his feet, and to have seen the end of his youthful follies. After more than a year of comfort and happiness there appeared on the scene some evil genius who had known his wife before her marriage, and began to give hints and innuendos of her former position. This came to the bishop's ears, and he sent for X. Y. and in the kindest manner told him how reluctant he was to believe the story, yet if it were true he had better resign his position, and thus try to put a stop to any unpleasantness. My friend told him frankly that the story was partly correct, but that now both he and his wife were *sans peur et sans reproche*, and rather than be shunned by his quondam friends he would resign his position at once, and leave the province. He did so, and went further west, and having only a small settled income he opened a school, which became fairly successful, and he thought he should soon recover his former position. He was suddenly struck down by fever and his life was despaired of, but owing to the perfect devotion and unremitting attention of his wife he recovered, with the terrible drawback that his wife took the infection and died, leaving him alone amongst strangers. No words could describe, he told me, the devoted love and affection his wife accorded him, and his heart was almost broken. He recovered his health sufficiently to return to England, and after an interview with his father commenced life anew. He succeeded in taking orders in the Episcopal Church of Scotland, and I heard a few years since that he was a careful, good priest in his new home, and deeply attached to his duties. He spoke with great concern of his altered circumstances, and said, 'These clothes I am now wearing were made by Poole, of Savile Row, and I have kept them carefully for high days and holidays, that I might, when requisite, keep up a good appearance.' Many a time have I ridden with him at the covert side, and seen him go as gallantly as any man during his undergraduate career. I dare say this is no isolated case, of a gay and popular young student of our leading Universities coming to so great a misfortune.

Amongst the most memorable events over the steeplechase course at the Prebendal Farm, Aylesbury, were the inter-University steeplechases. The horses had to be entered and ridden by members of the Universities of Oxford and Cambridge. Three horses were to be nominated by each University, and the following were the entries for the race run on March 26, 1863:

OXFORD

Mr. Frederick's The Dane, ridden by Mr. Mountain.
Mr. Rowe's Brown George, ridden by owner.
Mr. Oakton's Reindeer, ridden by Mr. Beach.

CAMBRIDGE

Mr. Wentworth's The Clown, ridden by owner.
Mr. Karrington's Gorilla, ridden by Mr. Forrester.
Mr. Wentworth's Conqueror, ridden by S. Oakton.

It was agreed that, as the former were accustomed to ride over the course, the race should be run the reverse way, so that practically the Oxford men had no advantage over their opponents. It is unnecessary to describe the race itself, as it contained the usual number of mishaps which characterise a cross-country meeting, but the point of most interest was the following: The Dane, considered one of the cleverest horses ever steered over a course, and the intended winner for Oxford, refused the fifth fence; from the start he was leading, and all the six horses were driven up in a heap and the favourite was pushed into the ditch. They then all turned round and went at the fence together. The Clown was first over, and made the rest of the running with a clear lead until near the finish, and as soon as Mr. Fitzwilliam, who rode under the assumed name of Wentworth, called on him to finish, he stood still, kicked and reared, and allowed Conqueror to pass him and win. Notwithstanding that Cambridge won the race, the Cantabs lost heavily, as they had all backed The Clown. The Oxford men were very crestfallen, and old Charlie Symonds, who was the real owner of The Dane, blew up Mr. Mountain for his bad riding. He offered to back The Dane single-handed against any horse the Cambridge men had, for any sum of money they liked, but they were afraid to take his offer. The race terminated thus, Cambridge winning everything:

Conqueror, 1; The Clown, 2; Gorilla, 3.

Two years afterwards, on April 5, 1865, the return match came off, when the following were the entries:

OXFORD

Mr. Stanhope's Kate, ridden by Mr. Ashby.
Mr. Buttevant's Loyalty, ridden by Mr. Johnson.
Mr. Leathes' Marchioness, ridden by owner.

CAMBRIDGE

Mr. Douglas's The Good Lady, ridden by Mr. Rowley.
Mr. Percy's Colleen Bawn, ridden by T. Wentworth.
Mr. T. Wentworth's Preposition, ridden by Mr. Cecil.
„   „   Hermitage, ridden by Mr. Douglas.

This was a slashing race, and the finish was as under:

Marchioness, 1 ; Hermitage, 2 ; Loyalty, 3.

I cannot quite remember the real names of the owners or riders, as it was considered unadvisable that the University authorities or their own parents even should know that they were riding races, but at this distance of time it is immaterial, and Mr. Hill, who was the nephew of Lord Hill, was named Mountain, and the Fitzwilliams were named after their house, 'Wentworth.' I remember that Mr. Lance was 'Mr. Dart,' and Mr. James Allgood, 'Captain Barlow,' and many of my readers will recognise the names at that time as very familiar in the Universities. It will be seen that the superiority of one or other of the great seats of learning had not been definitely settled, and I could never understand how it was that these rival contests were given up. To me these meetings had a special interest, as they gave me the infinite pleasure of making the acquaintance, and I hope I may say the friendship, of the Right Hon. James Lowther, who was one of the representatives of Cambridge, Mr. W. Beach, M.P., whose fall at my father's farm at Broughton, off The Dean, laid him up at the farmhouse for some considerable time, as also Lords Cork, Coventry, and many others of those stirring University times.

At the present day a great movement has taken place in steeplechasing owing to the introduction of 'point to point' races, but I feel sure it will soon fail, there is nothing original in it. The first steeplechases of fifty years ago were all 'point to point' races, which I have described in a former book of mine. I do not say I was the originator of the modern system, but I had long seen the folly of the old plan, because very few people could see the race, and even those men who were well mounted fared but little better than the foot people, and if they did see much of it they must constantly have been getting in the way of the riders, and the result was, that those who saw the start could scarcely, if ever, see the finish, and *vice versâ*; and when there was a difficult fence to be negotiated, or a good piece of water to be cleared, a certain number of spectators were assembled at that spot, and they really saw nothing else. As soon as I had anything to do with the management of a steeplechase, I determined that the general public should see it, and at the old Broughton country, which was over my father's farm, I arranged that the start and finish should be either in or near the same field, and that other points of interest should be generally visible to the public. When I became tenant of the Prebendal Farm at Aylesbury I was enabled to make a course which nearly every sportsman says is the best natural one in England. I also found out that to have an impracticable or a dangerous fence in the course, which was almost certain to throw a horse down, was an unsportsmanlike proceeding, as, irrespective of the danger, it spoilt the race, and a poor finish was generally the result. Many others besides myself had seen this failure to please the *habitués* of steeplechases, and had remedied the difficulties, and made the courses such as could be fairly well seen, and be safely ridden over; but the now general adoption of 'gate-money' meetings has completely superseded a *natural* course, and has given us made-up fences and artificial water jumps, sometimes filled by a water-cart on the morning of the race, and the really good, old-fashioned, seasoned hunter, such as is ridden by gentlemen in the shires, who go fairly well to hounds, has seldom a chance to win a big race. This fact was commented on in a conversation I once had with my old friend the late Charlie Symonds, of Oxford, who, in alluding to the present class of steeplechases, said:

Sometimes one of my hard-riding friends says to me, 'Charlie, I have just bought "a clipper," a real weight carrier, only six years old, nearly thoroughbred, and a perfect gentleman at his fences, by Jove! I think he's good enough to win the Liverpool.' Well, I go to see this clever animal in the hunting field. I see him perform, he seems perfect, and all that his owner represented him to be, and he is put into a local steeplechase to try what he can do. He comes to the post in the pink of condition, has a good man on him, gets a good start, and before he has gone a mile a smart-looking little hack gallops him to a standstill.

This is the effect of the modern style of course; many of the best of our steeplechasers of the present day are *race-horses* somewhat troubled with *the slows* at Newmarket, but are then trained to be quick and clever at their fences, and to race down the thoroughly good hunters that are justly renowned in the shires. Among the successful horses of old days I remember Old Vivian, Lottery, The Chandler, Consul, Vainhope, and

Grimaldi, and they were steered by such men as old Captain Beecher, Bill Bean, Jem Mason, W. Archer, Powell, and Dan Seffert, and by such amateur gentlemen riders as Lord Strathmore, the Marquis of Waterford, the Hon. Chandos Leigh, Jemmy Allgood H. Blundell, H. Allnutt, and Burton, all of whom I have seen ride gallant races, and have shown what could be done by careful riding, good judgment, and determined pluck over a stiff, fair hunting country. It is, however, wonderful how popular the modern steeplechases and hurdle races have become, and what pleasure the public in general take in seeing really good horsemanship, more especially on the part of ladies, and nowhere does a lady look so well and appear so fascinating as when on horseback. Although some people object to ladies riding across country, yet it would be hard lines to deprive them of the pleasure of finding themselves safely carried along after a good pack of hounds, and exciting as much admiration by the gracefulness of their horsemanship as ever they could in the whirling waltz in the ball-room or on the green sward of the lawn-tennis court. It was indeed a treat to see that peerless Empress of Austria attended on by poor 'Bay Middleton,' or to see the Hon. Mrs. Villiers piloted by Jem Mason, riding in the first flight in 'the Grafton,' or 'Selby-Lowndes' country, or as I have often seen those dashing ladies, not only in those countries, but after the Baron's hounds in the vale of Aylesbury. Their daring feats and resolute riding excited my warmest admiration, but alas! 'Anno Domini' will prevent my ever enjoying that pleasure again.

CHAPTER XVI

The Agricultural Labourer—Advantages of a Wooden Leg—Sermon on Optics—Short-horn Breeding—Bates and Booth Breeds—Mr. Adkins of Milcote—High Prices for Short-horns.

WITH many people it is a common reproach in speaking of the agricultural labourer that he is a stolid, opinionated, senseless blockhead ; but my experience is quite the reverse. With a certain amount of retiring shyness, there is a shrewdness and under-current of humour, and a keen appreciation of a good joke, rarely found in others of the working classes. I have heard, and already recorded, many stories which fully bear out these remarks, and the following anecdote contains a vein of true humour. My readers who are not agriculturists must understand that there are two systems of planting field beans, one by drilling with the ordinary field drill and the other by setting with the hand. In the latter method the man uses a line and has a dibber, with which he makes a hole in the ground with his right hand, and with his left he takes from a small bag hanging in front of him two or three beans, and drops them into the hole already made by the dibber ; and a dexterous workman will set or plant a bushel of beans on about a quarter of an acre of land by two o'clock in the afternoon, when his work is considered done for the day. One of my men said to me:

'Master, you should always have a wooden-legged man to go bean setting.' 'Yes,' I replied, 'I see that, because he could make a hole for the beans with his wooden leg.' 'Oh, no,' said he, 'it's not that; it's *to puzzle the crows*. Don't you see, sir, the old crows come down as soon as we leave off work, and would see the holes the wooden-legged man made, and would at once go to work pecking at the hole; and when they found no beans they would go to the next hole, and the next, and the next; and when they can't find any beans they would call out to their comrades and say, "This won't do; there's no beans in this field." And away they all would fly, and go to some one else's field. So you see, sir, you *should always have a wooden-legged man, if you can find one, to go a bean setting.*'

I am reminded by this of a capital story, which was told with great glee by the late Mr. Baily, the distinguished poulterer in Mount Street. A wooden-legged man of his acquaintance not only boasted of having a wooden leg, but said that it was the greatest blessing possible.

'For instance,' he said, 'I was one day going down a narrow street leading out of the Strand, and a cry arose of "Mad dog!" Everyone ran away, and I rushed into a house and shut the door, but not before the rabid animal had seized my leg and bit it very savagely. "Have it cauterised at once," said the owner of the shop. "Never mind," I said, "*it's only a wooden one.*" The most fortunate thing in the world is to have a wooden leg; if it hadn't been for that I should have died of hydrophobia. On another occasion I was going down one of the steep lanes leading to the Adelphi, and met a waggon heavily laden with coal. I unfortunately slipped up, and the waggon went over my leg. The driver was horrified, and cried out, "Send for a doctor and take him to the 'orspital!" "Never mind," I said; "send for a carpenter to bring a hammer and some nails; he'll soon put the broken leg to rights!" So you see it's a capital thing to have a wooden leg.

At another time I was at Brighton, and went out in a boat with three friends. The boat upset; my friends could not swim and were drowned. I floated on my back, took out my handkerchief, tied it on to my wooden leg, stuck it up in the air; the flag flew, a boat put off seeing the flag, and rescued me! So you see it's a famous thing to have a wooden leg. The only time it was ever unpleasant for me was when I was at a country inn and the chambermaid warmed my bed. Before I got into bed I told the girl to come and fetch my candle, and I forgot to unscrew and take off my wooden leg, which stuck out at the bottom of the bed. She came in and said, 'God bless me! I have left the warming-pan in the bed. The poor gentleman must be burnt." She caught hold of my wooden leg, and pulled me clean out of bed. So you see this was not very pleasant; but, after all, *it's a capital thing to have a wooden leg*.'

Another agricultural story is amusing. I must preface my tale by saying that in Hampshire and the adjoining counties hops are largely cultivated, and in this hop district, in a purely country village, the vicar of the parish was a great student on the structure of the human eye, and often gave lectures, and read learned papers at the Ophthalmic Society's meetings. On a certain Sunday, when he got into the pulpit, and pulled out what he thought was his sermon, he discovered that it was one of his lectures on 'Optics,' and, as might be well imagined, he was horrified, as he could not think what he should do. At last a happy thought struck him for the missing text, and he said, 'My Christian brethren, the text I am about to give you is so well known to you that it is immaterial to give you the reference, 'The eye of the Lord seeth all things.' He then with great solemnity read his lengthy paper on 'Optics,' and concluded by his reference to the text as being so peculiarly adapted to his discourse. When the service was over, as is often the custom in country parishes, the leading farmers and others waited outside the church to receive the kindly salutations of their vicar, and to exchange their views with each other; and one of the leading parishioners told the vicar what a capital sermon it was, and how much they all enjoyed it, 'but,' he said, 'I know you'll excuse me, sir, but there was one mistake as you made all through the sermon : you kept on calling 'em *hop sticks*, now all about here in this part of the country we always calls 'em *hop poles*.'

There is a sort of fascination for all Englishmen to dabble in country pursuits, more especially when they have sufficient capital to go in for farming, and, of all sorts of farming the most attractive seems to be the breeding of short-horn cattle, with the exception possibly of that most alluring pursuit, the breeding and rearing of thoroughbred horses. Thirty years ago nearly everybody thought it necessary to hire land, if they were not the owners of the broad acres themselves, and as opportunity arose bought pedigree short-horns. It is a mistake to suppose that only at the period I am now recording short-horn cattle had reached high prices, because in the beginning of this century, at the brother Collings' sale, the noted bull Comet made a thousand guineas ! and considerable sums were given by men like Mason, Booth, Bates, and Sir Charles Knightley ; but I shall not dilate too much on my favourite hobby, and shall merely state for the information of the uninitiated that the great rival lines of blood, at the time I mentioned, had settled down under the designation of the Bates and Booth men. The former line was cheifly composed of the Duchess, Cambridge Rose, and Waterloo tribes, and when the bulls from these lines were used on the Knightley cattle they created a breed of extraordinary merit. I mention this generally, to explain how these rival lines became the watchwords of the two parties, and it seemed a heinous sin in searching the herd-book for the pedigree of a Bates animal to find a cross, however remote, of a Booth bull. The Knightleys may have as many crosses of Bates as possible, but woe betide a cross of Booth. It may be well seen, therefore, with what keenness at a sale a pure animal would be sought after. Amongst the greatest admirers of this line of blood was Mr. Adkins, of Milcote, near Stratford-on-Avon, and so pure was his herd that Strafford, the auctioneer and the owner of the herd-book, named him the *Collings* of the modern short-horn world. He had a renowned line of Knightleys called the Charmers, and beautiful indeed they were—splendid milkers, with lovely countenances, regular breeders, and when no longer in use for the dairy were rapid producers of fine meat.

I was also a devoted partisan of this tribe, and it so happened that on one occasion I had a catalogue of a short-horn sale sent me from a place called Long Ashton, near Bristol, and I found, mixed up with a lot of very common and despised pedigrees, a mother and daughter of the purest Knightleys and of the comparatively rare line the Furbelows. One was an oldish cow named Wine, and her white daughter, two years old, named White Wine. As the auctioneer was a countryman unknown to short-horn fame, I concluded that no one probably knew anything about this sale, so I determined to go down and try to buy these two animals. The sale was the day after one of our Farmers' Club meetings in London, and during the day I went to Paddington and booked my place by the limited mail to Bristol, and said not a word to anyone, not even to my people at home, for fear the secret of the sale should leak out. I stole out of our club-room, and a cab took me to the station. I arrived at my destination about midnight. I ordered at the hotel an early breakfast, and a fly to take me to Long Ashton, a distance of about eight miles. On leaving my bedroom about eight o'clock—judge of my horror and alarm—I met full in the face, emerging from a bedroom opposite, Mr. Adkins! He glared at me, and in his jolly, good-natured manner said, 'You rascal, I know what brought you here.' I laughed, and he said, 'I wish I was back at Milcote,' and I replied, 'I wish I was back at Aylesbury.' 'Come along,' he said; 'let us have our breakfast, and we can share the fly together. I have no doubt these cattle are in poor condition; I shan't bid much for them. We had better act independently of each other. I shall be satisfied with the old cow, and you can have the young one.' The sale commenced, and on Wine entering the ring she was put in at twenty guineas, and the biddings went on slowly, Mr. Adkins being mixed up with the crowd, and unseen by me, as I was on the opposite side of the sale ring. As the cow was hanging at thirty guineas I bid thirty-five, to the astonishment of the company, none of the previous lots having made more than eighteen or nineteen guineas each. The biddings started again, and eventually the cow was sold at forty-five guineas. I then went up to Mr. Adkins and congratulated him on having bought her within her value. 'I have not bought her,' he said; 'I thought you were bidding, so I stopped.' 'Well, then,' I said, 'there are three Richmonds in the field to-day,' and to the astonishment of both of us we found the buyer was the Rev. Mr. Storer, of Helidon, in Northamptonshire, one of the staunchest supporters of the Fawsley line! Here was an end of all our secrecy, for the reverend gentleman was well known to both of us, and was a really good fellow. However, things went on quietly, with the young cattle making from fourteen to sixteen guineas each, and when White Wine came into the ring I started her at sixteen guineas. She very soon ran up to forty guineas, and when I bid fifty guineas a shout went up from the ring as though a Duchess had been put up at a thousand, and in the end I bought her for fifty-five guineas, and Mr. Adkins and my reverend competitor congratulated me on possessing the purest-bred Furbelow in England I have detailed this at some length in illustration of the determination of devoted breeders to get the purest and best blood at that time obtainable. Alas! those times are gone, and no more will the glass run on the biddings of hundreds and of thousands of guineas that were not uncommon at that time, but have now become reduced, so that where thousands were once bid only hundreds are bid now, and in place of hundreds only fifties and thirties; and I'm afraid the old prices will never return. It was very singular that after all my trouble, and after keeping this cow for three years, she never bred me a calf, and in the end she was sent to the butcher, and thus ended, I believe, this special branch of the pure Furbelows. In all my experience I doubt if I ever had a greater disappointment. At the death of Mr. Adkins I bought from his executors the whole of his herd, about thirty females, and gave a thousand guineas for them, and divided them with my neighbour and friend Mr. Joseph Robinson. I retained a little heifer calf a month old—a pure Bates animal, named Secrecy—and when nearly three years old she was sold to the late Lord Chesham for a hundred guineas, and at his sale two years afterwards Lord Fitzhardinge gave four hundred guineas for her, and with her progeny at that sale she totalled seven hundred and eighty-five guineas! The next year I went down to the Duke of Devonshire's sale at Holker and bought a yearling bull, Duke of Oxford the Twenty-sixth, giving four hundred and twenty guineas for him, and after using him on my own and Mr. Robinson's herd, he was sold at his sale nearly three years afterwards to Mr. Rigg for seven hundred guineas. These were indeed halcyon days for breeders of short-horns!

CHAPTER XVII

Tombstones and their Inscriptions—Some ancient—Illiterate Spelling—
A Citizen of Taunton—The Lee Monument, 1584—Clever and Learned
at Munich—Severe Inscription at Luton—John Wilkes's Gardener—
Lady O'Looney—Lockyer and his Pills, with others in St. Saviour's,
Southwark—Quarrendon Chapel and its wanton destruction.

I HAVE often intended to write a history of tombstones and their inscriptions, but up to the present have not found time to make such investigations as would enable me to do so. A thoroughly complete history would involve going back for many centuries, even to pre-historic times. One would have to study the sculptures of Nineveh and the hieroglyphics of Egypt, with the lithographs on Greek tombs and Roman sarcophagi, and even the Runic characters of our northern climes; so I must content myself by mentioning some that I have myself seen and copied. I would make the prefatory remark that few people having time to spare ever leave a town or village without visiting the parish church and churchyards, and they cannot fail to be struck with the varied memorials recorded of the silent dead. Some inscriptions describe in glowing and forcible terms the virtues of the occupant of that grassy mound, who was perhaps a meek and lowly

Christian, but the zeal of some enthusiastic relative has raised him to something even higher than a saint, and has not been content with asserting that he was the kindest husband, the best of fathers, the most charitable of men, the best of companions, and possessed of many other virtues, but that he was afflicted with divers diseases, and at last yielded up his spirit, glad to rid himself of the tortures of this world. Sometimes these personal descriptions assume a droll and ludicrous aspect ; and I trust that, in any quotation of inscriptions I may make, I may be acquitted of any seeming levity, as I really look upon it in a serious light, and cannot help being impressed in a much greater degree by the simplicity of pre-Reformation inscriptions to be found equally in our noblest cathedrals and in the humblest village church. I think there is something so impressively touching and so prayerful on many an ancient brass in the simple words :

> Of your charitie say an ave or a pater noster
> for the soul of John * * * * and Mary hys wyfe—
> The which John deceased * * * * and Mary * * * *
> On whose soules God have mercy, Amen.

How different is this to :

> Afflictions sore long time I bore
> Physicksians was in vain
> Till God did plese to give me ease
> And free me from my pane!

This learned and well-spelt inscription is to Edward Hall, 1842, in Bletchley churchyard, and I trust the erudite mason who chiselled this was not educated by a School Board. This churchyard abounds in exquisite

O

rural and ill-spelt poetry. Here is another to Charlotte Johnson, 1833 :

> The grave is a bed of roses
> When true believers it encloses
> When my Jesus left the Tomb
> He left a long and sweet perfume
> When the last Arkangel's trump shall sound
> O ; may I then in Christ be found.

Again, to Charles Johnson, 1826 :

> Weep not my wife and children dear,
> I are not dead but resteth here
> Releived from sorrow grief and pain
> We hope in heaven to meet again.

In Wingrave churchyard, near Aylesbury, is the following very curious and descriptive one, on Mary Lucas ; she died November 13, 1724, aged thirty years :

Here lieth one who had Rachel's fair face, and Leah's fruitful womb, Abigail's wisdom, and Lydia's faithful heart ; Martha's care, and Mary's better part, which shall never be taken from her.

> Oh ! hasty death and fleeting time
> To cross sweet flowers in there prime
> Scarcely ; staying tell they are blown—
> Or unto there perfection grown—
> Shure of her I unworthy was
> Short was her life soon run her glass.

In some is a mixture of poetry relative to the time of death, as in Eyam churchyard, Derbyshire :

Here lieth the body of Ann Sellars, buryed by this stone,
Who dyed on January 15, 1731.
Likewise here lise dear Isaac Sellars, my husband and my right,
Who was buryed on the same day come seven years, 1738.

> In seven years time there comes a change—
> Observe and here you'll see
> On that same day come seven years
> My husband's laid by me.

It will be seen that the above was intended to be a sort of poem, the first line ending in 'stone,' the second in 1731 (one), and in Derbyshire dialect it would be read seventeen hundred and thirty *ight* so as to rhyme with *right*.

In Fairford occurs this extraordinary couplet :

> Beneath this stone lie two children dear
> The one at Stony Middleton—the other here.

This place was about twelve miles from Fairford. How few of these inscriptions of the last century and the beginning of the present one raise our ideas to a purer or a better state ! and the wretched spelling of the chiseller destroys that which sometimes might be moderately decent. Take the following from Conisburgh, Yorkshire :

> Go home my wife and children dear
> I must lie hear till Christ apear
> And at his comeing I hope to have
> A joyful riseing from the grave.

In others the spelling is only equalled by the grammar, as at Farcet Church, Hunts, on Ralph Bradford, 1841 :

> Tho his affliction it was great
> And hath prepared him for a place
> God has him now releast
> Where joy are never ceased.

At St. Mary's, Scarborough :

> This world's a city full of crooked streets
> Death is the market place where all men meets
> If life where merchandies that men could buy
> Rich men would live and poor men die.

The next is from St. Mary's, Taunton, which I copied in 1845, to the memory of Robert Graye Esqr. and founder, Anno domini 1635 — Ætatis Suæ, 65 :

> Taunton bore him, London bred him
> Piety trained him—Virtue led him
> Earth enriched him, Heaven carest him
> Taunton blest him, London blest him
> This thankful town, that mindful city
> Share his piety, and his pity
> What he gave, and how he gave it
> Ask the poor, and thou shalt have it
> Gentle reader, Heaven may strike
> Thy tender heart to do the like
> Now thine eyes have read the story
> Give him the praise, and heaven the glory.

Aylesbury old church, dedicated to St. Mary, is a remarkably fine specimen of Early English architecture, and of late years most ably restored by Sir Gilbert Scott, who looked upon the restoration as a labour of love, as it was his county town, he told me, he having been born at the little village of Gawcott, near Buckingham, and his friendship it was my privilege to enjoy. In the north transept stands a tomb which had been sadly mutilated, and portions of it Sir Gilbert discovered to be of very fine alabaster, bearing date 1584, which was the period of the decadence of Gothic art; but many were, like this, of the Renaissance in particularly good taste, and even of beauty, but out of place in our glorious Gothic churches. This tomb was in memory of one of the Lees of Quarrendon, who are the same family as the Lees of Ditchley, of Kenilworth fame. It consists of a decorated canopy with shields, and covering two marble kneeling

THE LEE MONUMENT AT AYLESBURY

figures, nearly life size, and two very small figures in swaddling clothes. There are some introductory lines beneath the statues, as under :

> If passing by this tomb thou dost desire
> To know what in this marble shrine do lie
> The some of that which now thou dost require
> This sclēder verse to you will soon descrie.

The following inscription is quaint and quite Spenserian in its diction, and the spelling with its contraction and omission of the letter 'n' is peculiar, as follows :

> Entombed here doth lie a worthy dame
> Extract and born of noble house and blood
> Her sire Lord Paget hight of worthy fame
> Whose virtues cannot sinke in Lethe's flood
> Two brethren had she Barōs of this realm
> A Knight, her feere, Sir Henry Lee he hight
> To whom she bare three impes which had to name
> John, Henry, Mary slain by fortunes spight
> First two beīg young which caused their parēts mōe
> The third in flower and prime of all her yeares
> All three doe rest within this marble stone
> By which the fickleēss of worldly ioyes appears.
> Good friend sticke not to strew with crimsō flowers
> This marble stone wherein her cīdres rest
> For sure her ghost lives with the heavēly powers
> And guerdon hath, of virtuous life possest.

The words 'he hight' mean 'was his name,' and her 'feere,' her companion or husband. The letter 'n' is constantly left out, as mōe for 'mone.' It is also curious that the children are called 'impes,' probably meaning infants.

In Munich Cathedral is a remarkably clever inscription which requires considerable explanation. It must be understood that the word 'super' is omitted, but must be placed over some of the words:

O	quid	tua		
be	bis	bia	or superbe	superbis superbia
	te			
	avit		'or overcomes thee	
ra	ra	ra	three or ter	ra earth or dust
	es			
	et	in		
ram	ram	ram	three or ter	terram
	ii		i bis	

The translation would thus be, 'O proud man, why art thou so proud? Thy pride overcomes thee. Dust thou art, and into dust thou shalt go.'

An inscription very much amused me which I saw about ten years since on a slab in the north aisle of Luton churchyard:

> Here lies the body of Daniel Knight
> Who all my life time lived in spite
> Base flatterers sought me to undo
> And made me sign what was not true
> Reader beware, whene'er you venture
> To trust a canting false dissenter.
> He died   1756, aged   years.

I was somewhat curious to know something of Mr. Knight, and why he wrote such a scathing attack on his dissenting neighbours, and discovered that he was a deacon of the Baptists, who were building a new chapel, to which he was the principal donor, so various papers were put before him for his signature relating to the site and the contracts for building, which he innocently signed, and afterwards found that he had signed away nearly all his property, and made himself almost a beggar. He therefore left the fraternity, and wrote his own epitaph. The blanks were left open to be filled up after his burial.

I should like to be able to give some account of the celebrated John Wilkes, who lived in Aylesbury several years, and was for some time member of Parliament for that borough. He resided at the Prebendal House, close to the church, and the extensive ornamental grounds are separated from the churchyard by a massive brick wall, and on this wall is affixed a slab erected by Wilkes to the memory of his gardener, and the inscription is so elegant, and shows so well the refined classical feeling of the great demagogue, that I cannot refrain from alluding to it:

To the memory of John Smart, gardener, who died 16th November, 1754, aged 54 years.

Illum etiam lauri, illum etiam flevere myricæ.—*Virgil.*

Which I freely translate:

For him even the laurels, for him even the myrtles weep.

There is something to me peculiarly beautiful in this quotation, and possibly a special tribute to his merits as a gardener.

There are many amusing records of memorial inscriptions, most of them apocryphal. One is too good to be omitted:

Here lies the body of Lady O'Looney
Great niece to Burke commonly called the sublime—
She was bland, passionate, and deeply religious.

Also

She painted in water colours, and sent several pictures to the exhibition—she was first cousin to Lady Jones—

And of such are the kingdom of heaven.

But the most astounding piece of arrogant and presumptuous folly I have ever seen is in that beautiful church now undergoing a great restoration, I mean St. Saviour's, Southwark. The tomb is erected to a maker of pills, and is inscribed on a gorgeous marble monument, with a life-sized recumbent figure, being, I suppose, a portrait of himself. This pill-maker was yclept Lockyer, and he must have been either the Holloway or Beecham of his time. He pretended that his pills were made *from the rays of the sun.*

> Here Lockyer lies interr'd; enough, his name
> Speaks one hath few competitors to fame,
> A name so great, so gen'ral, it may scorn
> Inscriptions which do vulgar tombs adorn.
> A diminution 'tis to write in verse
> His eulogies, which most men's mouths rehearse
> His virtues and his pills are so well known
> That envy can't confine them under stone.
> But they'll survive his dust, and not expire
> Till all things else at th' universal fire.
> This verse is lost, his pills embalm him safe
> To future times without an epitaph.
>
> Deceased April 26, A.D. 1672. Aged 72.

Alas, poor Lockyer! your pills and yourself are forgotten. Perhaps like *Punch's* description of the death of 'Old Parr,' who died at the age, it is said, of 163, and who was killed by taking some of his own 'Life Pills,' the renowned Lockyer might have had a similar end, and yet I fear his pills did not actually embalm him.

I cannot refrain from quoting some more from this grand old church now under restoration, which when completed will be worthy of being the cathedral of the new see of Southwark. This is to Alderman Humble, about the year 1620, and is by some attributed to Beaumont :

> Like to the damask rose you see
> Or like the blossom on the tree,
> Or like the dainty flower in May,
> Or like the morning of the day,
> Or like the sun or like the shade,
> Or like the gourd which Jonah had ;
> Even so is man, whose thread is spun,
> Drawn out and cut and so is done !
> The rose withers, the blossom blasteth ;
> The flower fades, the morning hasteth,
> The sun sets, the shadow flies,
> The gourd consumes, the man he dies.

This church has several other quaint and curious inscriptions. One which I copied recently is peculiar in the remarkable division of the words :

> Nicholas Norman
> Waterman late
> Servant to the
> King's Maiestie and
> Elizabeth his wife
> were here buryed
> Hee the 25th of May
> 1629—and shee the
> 15th of Januarie fol
> lowing who li
> ved 16 years to
> gether in the Ho
> lie state of Matr
> imonie and dœ here
> rest in hope of a ioy
> full resurrection.

In a monument on a wall is another to William Austin, Esq., 'who in contemplation was an angel ; in action a Dædalus ; in travel as good as a conveyance ;

at table a feast in himself; a miracle of patience; in death a pattern of faith.' After such stuff as this, a little child, in reading this class of inscription in a churchyard, might well ask her father 'where all the bad people were buried.'

Whilst writing of the restoration of St. Saviour's, Southwark, I cannot refrain from mentioning the disgraceful condition in which some of our parish churches are left—not only in a state of decay, but of absolute wilful ruin. I can quite understand why many of our beautiful ancient abbeys remain in ruins, as the actual need of them in the present day no longer exists, and when I hear from sextons and parish clerks in charge of our churches and cathedrals that the author of their destruction and desecration was Cromwell, they not only believe it themselves, but persuade their hearers also, that it was 'Oliver' of that ilk who is responsible. They seem to be unaware that, iconoclast as he undoubtedly was, and often as he had stalled his horses in our finest ecclesiastical buildings—thus turning them into stables, and even the chancel into barracks for his soldiery—it will be found that he destroyed little indeed in comparison with his namesake, 'Thomas, Lord Cromwell,' who boasted, in his returns to his royal master, Henry VIII., of the number of abbeys and monasteries he had destroyed, with other religious houses, and the serious injury he then caused remains to this day; but his retribution was near at hand, for the Great Harry in the end cut off his Lordship's head. We know under what circumstances these acts were perpetrated, but it is scarcely credible that, in the nineteenth century, such devastation and sacrilegious destruction could take place as I have myself seen in the parish of Quarrendon, not three miles from Aylesbury. The beautiful old church, or chapel-of-ease to the adjoining parish of Bierton, is now a ruin, and its destruction has taken place within living memory, and those in authority, to their shame be it said, calmly and complacently, by their unpardonable inaction, apparently acquiesced in it. Quarrendon is a parish of over two thousand acres, of the richest pasture land in the Vale of Aylesbury, and it is the favourite home and feeding-ground of the white-faced Hereford ox and the Leicester sheep. It is said that it was the birthplace of Offa, king of Mercia, and there is but little doubt that his daughter, St. Osyth, was born there. She founded a nunnery at Aylesbury, and, taking with her some devoted women, founded another on the banks of the Thames. She received the crown of martyrdom from the Danes, and her shrine became famous near London. Her name is still perpetuated in the City by 'Size Lane,' a corruption of *St. Osyth's* Lane. Quarrendon Chapel stands in a grass field, and close to it are the remains of a large and important mansion, and the earthworks of a 'keep' with a double fosse round it; these were probably of a very early date. Afterwards it became the residence of the Lee family, who were noted people in the Middle Ages, to whom I have already alluded in describing their tomb in Aylesbury Church. When I first saw this church, fifty years ago, there then existed some remarkably handsome tombs in the chancel, but there was no roof left on any part of the building, nor was there a window or a door in the place. When I visited it there were eight or ten great Hereford oxen sheltering themselves from the sun in the nave, and the chancel was hurdled off for sheep. Men were then living who remembered marriages being celebrated in the church, and an occasional service performed by the clergyman from Bierton. Quarrendon was in the diocese of Lincoln and archdeaconry of Buckingham, and the presentation to the living belonged to the Prebend of Lincoln, and was a chapel-of-ease to the parish of Bierton. The landowner of all the parish was Mr. Du Pré, who resided at Beaconsfield, about twenty-five miles distant. There were only five tenant-farmers residing in the parish, and one labourer, who called himself clerk and sexton. It will thus be seen that everyone was interested in permitting this church to fall into ruin. It was a beautiful specimen of architecture, representing the transition period from Decorated to Perpendicular, and had remains of great interest. When one of the tenants required a gatepost a beam was taken from the roof, while the lead from the roof had been appropriated some time ago—'conveyed, the wise it called,' and when railings to mend a fence were wanted many rafters were carried off. When the farmyards, cowhouses, or gateways required stoning, part of a wall was pecked down and carted away, and occasionally the roads also were mended with its ruins. This is no exaggeration, and I can vouch for the following as a fact. I was one day visiting a highly respectable and very intelligent farmer in the parish, who lived about half a mile distant, and who was telling me of some improvements he was carrying out in his garden. He said he was going to build a summer-house near the brook running through his grounds, and make it a sort of ruin, and that he could get two or three windows and other ornamental stonework from the chapel and one of the doorways, and build them into the walls, and when covered with ivy, it would look very well. I expressed my horror at his suggestions, and he replied that it might just as well be used for that purpose as to repair the cow-sheds and pig-styes, &c.; and surely enough when I visited the place a few months afterwards, there was the summer-house, built from the ancient structure once dedicated to the service of Almighty God, and used for many centuries for that purpose. But this is nothing to what I can also vouch for. There was a man residing in Aylesbury, who was a turner by trade, and a leading part of his business was making ornamental marble candlesticks, which were at that time popular decorations for the mantel-shelf; and this worthy was accustomed to go to Quarrendon Chapel, when he had an order, *and break off a leg or an arm from the alabaster figures of the Lee monuments, and then turn them with his lathe into candlesticks*, for which he had a ready sale. I once saw a leg broken off in this manner, with the garter in rich blue enamel and the legend in gold letters, 'Honi soit qui mal y pense' still visible. No one attempted to prevent the barbarous destruction of this interesting building. The Prebendaries of Lincoln drew their emoluments from the parish, caring nothing for so distant a place. The landlord saved finding timber for repairs, the farmers got rid of rates for the protection and maintenance of their church, and found the building to be a good timber-yard and stone-quarry for their daily use, and ' God's acre,' or burial ground, made a convenient paddock for general service. But above all the Bierton parson was glad to get rid of the trouble of walking or riding three miles to perform the Sunday service, for which he was duly paid. I yield to no man in my devotion and love for the Anglican Church, and in admiration and respect for the country gentry, but no expressions of mine can be too strong in condemning the conduct of the authorities of the Church, nor the apathy and neglect of the landlord for allowing so disgraceful an act of sacrilege as this. Nor should the farmers escape censure; their conduct was as reprehensible as that of the landlord. This beautiful ruin still remains as a specimen of gross neglect and indifference to a sacred edifice, and the churchyard is thrown open to the depredations of cattle, and other live stock.

During my wanderings through the county I have sometimes come upon remarkably old trees, many of them evidently of great antiquity and occasionally of historic interest. It has often struck me that they are really connected with some important event—take, for instance, the Boscobel oak which hid Charles II., and during her Majesty's reign many have been planted with her own hands, and will eventually be referred to with much interest. Some years ago I went to see an oak tree that had been shown to me in my childhood, which was called 'Waller's Oak,' and, when I saw it, it was still vigorous and flourishing. This celebrated tree is growing at Coleshill, a small hamlet near

Amersham, in a field called Stock Place, where there was a house which was tenanted for some years by members of my family. This wonderful tree is considered by many persons to be the largest in girth of any oak in the kingdom. When I was there I measured it, and found its trunk was forty-five feet in circumference just above the ground, and its gnarled branches covered a space of two hundred feet round. It is quite hollow, and only a mere shell, but still vigorous and green. It had its historical and poetical associations, as there was a niche cut in the tree, in which it was stated the courtly Waller was accustomed in the summer-time to sit and write his poems, in the time of the second Charles. It must have been a famous tree even at that time, and I have but little doubt it existed at the time of the Conquest, or perhaps even earlier as a Druidical oak, as it 'stands in its pride alone' in this small field, with no trees near it, and only hedgerows of whitethorn and wildbriar, which makes it conspicuous, besides the fact that Coleshill is on very high ground—I believe about eight hundred feet above the sea. Many visitors were in the habit of cutting off branches and chopping away portions of the trunk, and carrying them off as mementos of their visit, but Mr. Drake, to whom the property belongs, has now inclosed it with an iron railing, and thus protects it. My visit here led me to make inquiries as to Waller's association with this place, and I find, in consulting Johnson's 'Lives of the English Poets,' in vol. i. p. 258, he gives an account of the poet's death, which is so interesting that I am forced to quote it:

Edmund Waller was born at Coleshill [I have always been told in the small house tenanted by my uncle]. His father was Robert Waller, Esq., of Agmondesham [Amersham], in Bucks, whose family was originally a branch of the Kentish Wallers ; and his mother was the daughter of John Hampden, of Hampden, in the same county, and was sister to Hampden, the Zealot of the rebellion. Towards the decline of his life he bought a little land at Coleshill, and said 'he should be glad to die, like an old stag in his lair, where he was roused.' This, however, did not happen. When he was at Beaconsfield he found his legs go tumid ; and went to Windsor, where Sir Charles Scarborough then attended the king, and requested him, as a friend and a physician, to tell him *what that swelling meant*. 'Sir,' answered Scarborough, 'your blood will run no longer.' Waller repeated some lines of Virgil, and went home to die. As the disease increased upon him, he composed himself for his departure ; and calling upon Dr. Birch to give him the last Sacrament, he desired his children to take it with him, and made an earnest declaration of his faith in Christianity. It now appeared what part of his conversation with the great could be remembered with delight. He related that being present when the Duke of Buckingham talked profanely before King Charles, he said to him, ' My Lord, I am a great deal older than your Grace, and have, I believe, heard more arguments for Atheism than ever your Grace did ; but I have lived long enough to see there is nothing in them, and so I hope your Grace will.' He died October 21, 1687, and was buried at Beaconsfield, with a monument, erected by his son's executors, for which Rymer wrote the inscription.

I revisited Stock Place about two years since with my esteemed friend and kinsman, Mr. Thomas Grove, J.P., who resides on the old family estate of Penn, which has been in the possession of their family ever since the Conquest, the manor of which was granted by William the Conqueror to one of his trusty soldiers, Sir Edmund de Grove, who was knighted by him after the battle of Hastings. Waller's family mansion was 'Hall Barn,' close to Beaconsfield, bought a few years ago, and now tenanted by the owner, Sir Edward Lawson, Bart. It is a remarkably stately house, built in the then prevalent style of architecture, and stands in very extensive ornamental grounds, and surrounded by a large landed property. The mansion has been much added to by Sir Edward, and is a model of external and internal decoration. Waller must have lived in close proximity to Milton, who wrote 'Paradise Lost' at Chalfont St. Giles, about three miles distant, and about the same distance off lies Stoke Poges, celebrated by Gray's 'Elegy in a Country Churchyard.' I believe Waller sat in one parliament for the borough of Amersham.

CHAPTER XVIII

A terrible Parricide—Singular Evidence—Fitzroy Kelly and the Missing Pocket-book—Adding 'Fuel to fire'—The Verdict—Chequers Court and the Kimbles—Similarity of Pedigree of Charles I. and Cromwell —Anne Hyde, Mother of Two Queens—Reminiscences of Jockeys— Old Bob Barker.

SOME years ago the perpetration of a terrible tragedy shocked the neighbourhoods of Aylesbury and Leighton Buzzard. A yeoman farmer, whose name I forbear to mention, resided a few miles from the latter town, and was a man in a good position, but with a bad temper, and had made himself much disliked by his numerous family, and also by his neighbours. One evening he was seen walking round his farm, and as he had not come home when night closed in, his wife became alarmed, and the farm buildings and fields adjoining were searched, but no trace of him could be found. His eldest son and the shepherd said they had seen him in a distant part of the farm near a cowhouse; and the next morning a closer examination was made, still no tidings were forthcoming. This son, then about twenty years of age, superintended the operations, but nothing was discovered; and it was afterwards remarked as being somewhat singular that the son had said it was useless to search the cowhouse, as he had been last seen in a contrary direction ; however, some of the men went there, and found the body concealed under some loose hay, with a fearful gunshot wound at the back of the head, and the brain was exposed. The body was removed to the house, and an inquest was held. At length suspicion fell upon the son, who, with the shepherd, was last seen in his company ; moreover, he had a gun in his hand, with which, he said, he was shooting small birds, who were damaging the corn, and he stoutly asserted his innocence. He was a well-educated, good-looking, inoffensive young man, but known to be a wildish fellow when in Leighton Buzzard on market day. Soon after the murder he was recklessly spending his money, after having changed a 5*l.* note at a local bank, which note was afterwards proved to have been one of two notes given to the father in exchange for a cheque by the bank. This seemed to make out a case of grave suspicion against him ; but he accounted for the possession of the note by saying that his father had given it to him on the morning of the murder. The crime took place, I think, in January, and the son was committed to take his trial at the assizes at Aylesbury, which was then on the Norfolk circuit and was the first place on the circuit. The greatest excitement prevailed, the trial lasting two days, and the court was filled to suffocation each day, with, as usual, a large proportion of ladies ; this is generally the case when any exciting trial is taking place, especially when it is for murder. Mr. Fitzroy Kelly, afterwards Lord Chief Baron, and the leader on circuit, was specially engaged to defend the prisoner, and I think Mr. O'Malley appeared for the prosecution.

A great deal of circumstantial evidence, as is generally the case in murder cases, was given, but the evidence was by no means strong enough for a conviction. Such was the highly reprehensible system of prison discipline at that time, that all the prisoners, whatever their crime, who were to be tried at the assizes were herded together in one ward in the day-time, and at night, although they had separate beds, they were all together in one dormitory. It so happened that a man named Fuell, who was awaiting his trial for burglary, came up to give evidence; and he deposed that the prisoner had confessed to him, whilst in gaol, that he had quarrelled with his father, who would not give him some money that he had asked him for. On the evening in question they were walking towards the cowhouse, and the prisoner was walking behind, and when the muzzle of his gun was close to the collar of his father's coat he pulled the trigger, and the contents entered his head, and his father fell dead. He then pulled him by his legs, face downwards, into the building, and, having satisfied himself that life was extinct, he covered him over with loose hay, having first taken his pocket-book with some loose money from his pockets, the book containing two 5*l.* notes; he then left the body and, having taken out the notes, placed the empty pocket-book under the thatch of an out-house near the dairy in the garden at the back of their residence. A few days after this story had been told to Fuell by the prisoner he thought it might be advantageous to him to divulge it, and so obtain for himself a more lenient sentence for his burglary. Consequently he told the story to Mr. Sherriff, the governor of the county prison, and a constable was sent soon after to search the building for the missing pocket-book, but nothing could be found, nor was there any trace of its having been placed there. Mr. Fitzroy Kelly, in addressing the jury for the defence, made a most powerful and eloquent speech, and contended that there was no direct evidence against the prisoner, who was a mild, inoffensive youth, and utterly incapable of committing so cruel and so diabolical an act of parricide, that this felon's evidence should be at once discarded, for there was not an atom of confirmation ; and that the main point on which the prosecution relied was the stealing of the pocket-book with the notes, which was entirely uncorroborated ; that this man's evidence was like adding ' fuel ' to fire, and there was nothing else to prove his guilt, as the pocket-book had not been found in the place indicated. He concluded a powerful speech by imploring the jury not to send this innocent youth to the scaffold. It was after nine o'clock at night when the judge commenced summing up, and the jury retired and returned into court a little before midnight, and amidst breathless silence returned a verdict of NOT GUILTY. And the youthful prisoner left the dock to join a lot of roystering young men, and returned home the next morning. The verdict surprised most people, and it was only the masterly address of Mr. Fitzroy Kelly that saved him from the gallows. Now comes the extraordinary sequel to this parricidal murder. A few days afterwards the prisoner was arrested and brought before the magistrates to answer the charge of robbing the dead body of his father, by stealing the two 5*l*. notes ;

and at the following assizes he was tried for this crime, found GUILTY, and he was sentenced to transportation for seven years. The jury never hesitated a minute in this case; the verdict, of course, was tantamount to finding him guilty of murder. I was present and heard the first trial, and like the majority of all who heard it believed in the guilt of the prisoner. I was intimately acquainted with his brother-in-law, who was a highly respectable farmer. He told me after the son had been transported that, as soon as the family heard of the confession, and the hiding of the pocket-book, he himself went off to the place indicated, found the pocket-book empty, exactly as it had been described by Fuell, and destroyed it, and thus prepared the ground-work of Kelly's defence. They kept this secret, as the family could not but feel horrified at the disgrace of their brother being hung on the gallows, much as they knew he deserved it. The young man served his full time of transportation abroad, and came back to this country, much broken in health, and died about a year afterwards of rapid consumption. He was very penitent, and fully confessed that he, and he alone, committed the terrible crime of shooting his unsuspecting father in a moment of unjustifiable anger. There was, I regret to say, a morbid desire to visit the place where the body was found, and for some time afterwards numbers of persons made *pleasure trips* to the spot, and probably took away some memento of the crime.

Chequers Court, Ellesborough, is the ancient seat of the Russells, but they are not to be confounded with the Bedford Russells, whose old family residence is at

'Chenies,' in the same county of Bucks. The mansion is a very picturesque structure, and is situated on the highest part of the Chiltern Hills, with beautiful flower gardens, and is surrounded by a well-timbered park, and a background of beech woods. A large conical hill shuts off the view of the Vale of Aylesbury, and at its feet is the far-famed 'Velvet Lawn,' the favourite picnic grounds of the population for twenty miles around. A great peculiarity of the hill slopes are the dense box woods which stretch for some miles, and are really beautiful at all seasons of the year. On the south-east foot of the hill is a very perfect ancient British camp, of undoubted authenticity, and was formed by Cymbeline, the king of Britain, when Julius Cæsar first invaded this country, 55 years B.C. Chequers Court was the country seat of the Russells in the early part of the seventeenth century, and the wife of the then owner was the favourite daughter of Oliver Cromwell; the Protector was a constant guest there, and at times almost made it his residence. It was only three miles from Hampden House, the home of the great patriot John Hampden; one can well believe that the two were often in close communication with each other. The town of Aylesbury, which is seven miles distant, was strongly Parliamentarian, and was notoriously badly affected towards the king; and in a former book of mine I have related a curious circumstance of the escape of the Earl of Rochester, after the battle of Worcester, and it is believed Oliver was at that time living at Chequers Court, and was most indignant at the escape of the Earl. I was greatly astonished, a short time since, at reading in Jesse's 'Court of the Stewarts' a pedigree of Oliver Cromwell, which is generally believed to be correct, that the 'Protector' and the King were of the same origin, and the line of blood, although somewhat altered by marriage, was identical. As this is not generally known, I venture to transcribe it here:

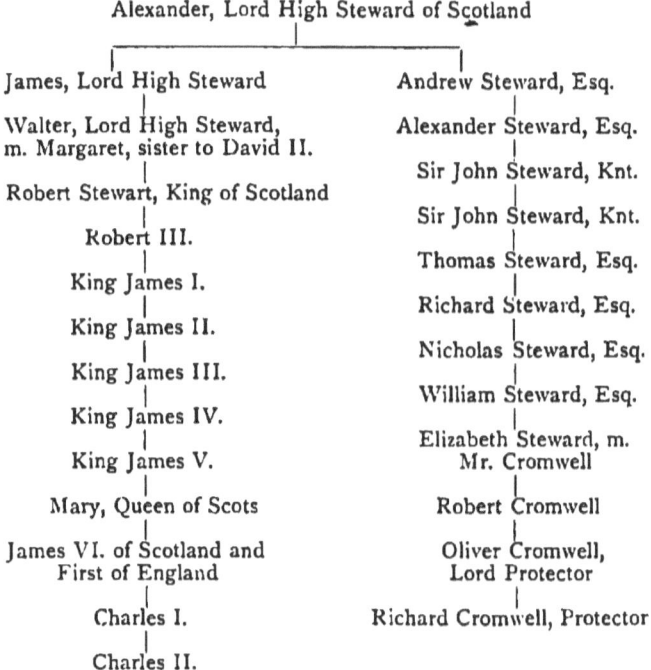

Alexander, Lord High Steward of Scotland

James, Lord High Steward	Andrew Steward, Esq.
Walter, Lord High Steward, m. Margaret, sister to David II.	Alexander Steward, Esq.
Robert Stewart, King of Scotland	Sir John Steward, Knt.
Robert III.	Sir John Steward, Knt.
King James I.	Thomas Steward, Esq.
King James II.	Richard Steward, Esq.
King James III.	Nicholas Steward, Esq.
King James IV.	William Steward, Esq.
King James V.	Elizabeth Steward, m. Mr. Cromwell
Mary, Queen of Scots	Robert Cromwell
James VI. of Scotland and First of England	Oliver Cromwell, Lord Protector
Charles I.	Richard Cromwell, Protector
Charles II.	

I am not aware of any record that the 'Protector' was cognisant of this relationship.

When reading this book of Jesse's at the public library at Twickenham, I saw in the margin of one of the pages, and continued on the blank page at the end of the chapter, from whence the above was taken, that some one had written in bold hand the following extraordinary statement :

'Anne Hyde, Duchess of York, wife of James II., was the eldest daughter of the great Lord Clarendon, and the mother of two Queens ; she was born in 1638.'

The mother of Anne Hyde was a pot-girl ; the troubles under Charles I. drove her from Brentford, where she was in service, to the town of Warminster, where she was employed to carry beer, then drawn from the cask, to those who had ordered it. After being in service four or five years her mistress died, and her master, finding her useful and clever, married her. She was his wife only a few years, when he died, leaving her a widow well off. She had occasion to consult a lawyer, a Mr. Hyde, then practising in the Temple. He, finding that she was a prosperous woman with property, married her. Hyde afterwards became Lord Chancellor with the title of Lord Clarendon, and his wife, the former pot-girl, bore him a daughter, who was married to the Duke of York, and became the mother of Mary and Anne Stewart, both afterwards queens of England. Thus it comes about that a pot-girl was the grandmother of two queens of England. The obscurity has been carefully preserved—Miss Strickland never alludes to it, but the facts are well known and never contradicted. Who was the grandmother of Mary and Anne Stewart ? And whom did Lawyer Hyde marry ?

There is a good story told of William Penn, who came from the village of Penn in my county, who afterwards founded Pennsylvania. When Penn was introduced to Charles II. he kept his hat on, in accordance with the custom of Quakers. The king took his own hat off. 'Friend,' quoth Penn, 'why dost thou not keep thy hat on?' ''Tis the custom of this place,' said the witty monarch, '*for only one person to remain covered at a time.*'

Waller, whom I have before alluded to wrote a splendid ode to Cromwell, and afterwards a wretched one to Charles, and on being asked by the king, 'Why it was?' said, 'Your Majesty knows that poets always deal best in fiction.' It is useless to allude to the profligacy of the times in England, but the state of France was even worse, and I give the following anecdote as an instance of the wit and immorality of the times. Cardinal de Rohan was, as is well known, a devoted follower of the Countess de Brienne. During a quarrel with her in her bedroom, she threatened to have him thrown out of the window. The cardinal replied that he could well afford *for once* to leave her chamber by the way he had so many times entered it.

I have known and seen some curious people, with many strange riders at our Aylesbury steeplechases, which I have had for many years to superintend as honorary clerk of the course; I have had the pleasure of the friendship of and social intercourse with many gentlemen and professional jockeys. There was a well-known rough customer, Old Bob Barker, at a certain race meeting of the 'Aylesbury Aristocratic,' when the course was at Broughton, and Old Bob rode a horse of Joe Tollit's called Tipperary Boy, which was one of the handsomest horses and finest jumpers I ever saw. After running nearly a mile the horses had to go round a tree, and return over nearly the same line ; this tree

THE OLD MARKET-PLACE, AYLESBURY, PULLED DOWN 1864

was in a large twenty-acre grass field ; there were ten or twelve horses running, and the late Tom Ball, who was one of the most elegant and finished horsemen that ever crossed a country and was huntsman to Baron

Rothschild, was riding one of the baron's horses in the race. He had turned round the tree, and was going a splitting pace, when Old Bob came thundering along, and, without attempting to avoid Tom Ball, rode fairly at him, collided, and both horses were knocked down. The latter was much shaken, but kept hold of the reins, and, was able to remount, whilst Barker was apparently senseless, and his horse got away. Some people ran to assist, helped Old Bob on to his legs, and one of them sympathised with him in his misfortune. Bob looked hard at him, and said, 'I don't want any of your sympathy; catch my d——d horse.' This was a sample of his rough and morose character.

A very amusing event happened the next day in the Broughton country, but over an entirely different course, when Barker was riding a very clever animal. He so punished him, however, that when the horse had run nearly two and a half miles, and was about a mile from home, he fell over a fence into a ploughed field. He was not much hurt, but Old Bob lay on the soft ground apparently severely injured. He appeared to be speechless, and some farm labourers and the usual loafers at a steeplechase fetched a hurdle, picked the poor injured fellow up, and put him on it, and with great difficulty and much labour carried him over some heavy ploughed fields, and brought him into the winning field, which adjoined my father's farmhouse. A doctor was in waiting and stimulants were ready when the old ruffian arrived; many of the gentlemen present got round him, when he suddenly jumped up, after being gently lowered to the ground, and walked off with

A JOCKEY'S GRATITUDE

nothing whatever the matter with him. Some one asked him how it was that after his severe fall he did not seem much hurt. 'Well,' he said, 'when I can find a set of d——-d fools ready to carry me a mile over a heavy country, I wasn't such a fool as to walk.' And this was the rider's gratitude to the poor men for carrying an apparently dying man, as they thought, off the course. This is fortunately a rare instance of discourtesy in steeplechase riders, either gentlemen or professionals; but I have not recounted these anecdotes as being typical of the class, for all the jockeys I have ever known, except Bob Barker, have been conspicuous for their quiet, gentlemanly conduct, and strict humanity to the noble animals they have ridden.

CHAPTER XIX

Agricultural Visits to the Continent—Manufacture of Sugar from Beetroot—Farming at Genappe and Waterloo—Ireland as a field for Sugar—Dr. Shack Sommer—Statistics of Saccharine—Percentage in Roots—Clarendon, Greville, and Thackeray on the Irish Peasantry—Dean Hole on Roses—Sappho and the Rose—Royal Agricultural Show at Windsor - Jubilee Life Members—Sixty years' Retrospect.

MY visits to the Continent as a judge at various agricultural meetings have been the source of much pleasure to me, and have enabled me to form some opinion on, and to make some comparison between, our systems of culture and those abroad, and I have always returned home with the pleasing conviction that we are much ahead of every European country in the superiority of our live stock, and of the machinery we use for the due cultivation of the land. In many parts of Germany, Austria, France, and Belgium the farmers have very materially improved their condition by turning their attention to the growth of white Silesian beetroot for the production of sugar. In every instance the result has been a triumphant success. Throughout the Continent there is scarcely a hundredweight of cane sugar consumed, and I have lately discovered that 75 per cent. of the sugar consumed in the United Kingdom is made from beetroot. I have given great attention lately

SUGAR FROM BEETROOT

to an examination of the cultivation of this valuable product. Before entering into a detail of this most interesting and important industry, I may say that about twenty-five years ago an attempt to grow white Silesian beet for sugar production was tried on a rather small area near Lavenham, in Suffolk, and Mr. Duncan, who was then the largest refiner in England, built a small factory for the manufacture and refining of sugar. I went down there with two of my neighbours from the Vale of Aylesbury, who had large farms, and who were experienced growers of mangel-wurzel, to see the factory, and we returned fully impressed with the certainty that this new departure in agriculture could be profitably carried out ; and, as I was confident that the first thing to do was to procure good seed, I wrote to the most eminent seedsmen in Belgium and the north of France to send me the best selected seed possible. The next year I planted five acres, and I had an excellent, well-harvested crop. In the meantime, I regret to say that, owing to the duty of twopence per pound being put upon all sugar, and from the apathy of the farmers around Lavenham, Mr. Duncan was unable to get sufficient roots to profitably employ all his machinery. He therefore gave up the factory, and my scheme fell through, and I had several hundredweight of seed left on my hands, as it became utterly unsaleable. I had published in the papers the results of my experiments, which created some interest at the time, and, because I still felt that the practice was feasible, I gave much attention to the subject whenever I was on the Continent. When I was elected president of the jury at the International Agricultural Exhibition at Brussels, about five years ago, I was invited to stay at the house of M. Van Volxhelm, at Genappe, on the plains of Waterloo. He had a fine farm of 250 acres, and possessed the second largest sugar factory in Belgium. I had then an opportunity of learning something of this great business. He told me the machinery and buildings there cost upwards of 40,000*l.* ; they were of the most improved character. My visit was in the middle of June, and, as the actual manufacture could not be carried on except in the months of November, December, and January, I could not see the process at work, but I had seen the system of culture and of the extraction, and had it explained to me by the courtesy of M. Van Volxhelm. I was much struck with the fine crops of all sorts on his farm, and expressed my astonishment, and he said, 'You may well be astonished, as the crops are growing in the bodies and remains of English and French soldiers, who fell around here at the battle of Waterloo; and the soil requires but little manure even now.' I came away with the full determination to try to persuade my English friends to turn their attention to the growth of this valuable root. Rather more than two years since a gentleman connected with a large Liverpool sugar refinery asked me to visit Ireland and report on 1,500 acres of what is called there 'slob land,' which had been reclaimed about five years before from the mouth of the river Fergus, which falls into the Shannon near the town of Ennis. In company with Dr. Shack Sommer, closely connected with the firm of Messrs. Crossfield & Barrow, sugar refiners of

Liverpool, I went over the 'distressful counthry,' and was much impressed with the suitability of the district for the growth of the sugar beet. Negotiations were opened up with Mr. Balfour, and afterwards with Mr. Jackson, who had succeeded him, for the purchase of the land from the Government, and arrangements were being pushed forward to commence operations in the ensuing year, when a storm arose of unexampled severity, and although the embankments and sluice-gates were very substantial, and the works were considered perfect, this tempest broke through one portion, and in a few hours the whole of the land was submerged and all our labour was lost. But, nothing daunted, we recommenced our operations, and this year—1893—we have thirty-seven places in various parts of England, eight in Ireland, and seven in Scotland, where carefully selected seed has been sent, and at present I am informed the most satisfactory results have been achieved. It has generally been considered that the climate of both England and Ireland is unsuited for the production of saccharine, but it has been proved to be quite the reverse. From a series of experiments, carefully carried out and tabulated, we get the following results. The percentage of sugar to a hundred parts of juice extracted from roots grown in the following years are as under:

In the Year	England	Scotland	Ireland	Germany	France
1889	15·76	—	17·55	16·39	15·51
1890	12·61	12·1	11·69	16·02	15·02
1891	13·21	12·88	13·48	15·95	14·38
1892	12·32	13·91	14·52	16·56	14·32
1893	14·21	14·56	15·10	15·42	15·66

It will be seen that there is ample proof that beetroot for sugar production can be grown to compete fairly with the Continent, as anything like an average of over 12 per cent. will pay well. There are, moreover, competent analytical chemists engaged in testing the quality of this year's roots, and it is expected that the result will be wonderful. The white Silesian beet, when grown by me twenty-five years ago, only yielded about 9 per cent. of sugar, but such has been the improvement in the production of saccharine since then by careful selection of roots for seed that the ratio has been increased by more than 5 per cent., and the difference has now made the growth of this root very profitable. I have many opportunities of talking to German, French, and Belgian agriculturists, and they agree with me that the growth of sugar beet in this country will be the solution of the difficulties attending the prosperity of British agriculture. The landowners must take up the subject, and put their hands in their pockets to establish one or two factories in different parts of England, and also in Ireland, and erect a factory perfect in all parts, with modern machinery, in a suitable spot, and urge their tenants to supply the factory with a plentiful quantity of roots. To make the factory pay the supply annually of roots should not be less than twenty thousand tons, which would require about twelve hundred acres to produce—*i.e.* about fifteen or sixteen tons to the acre—and the price should be 1*l*. per ton delivered, or about 15*l*. per acre, which is more than double the amount that any grain crop would yield. There is a further advantage, that after the sugar has been extracted the pulp can be used most favourably for feeding cattle and fattening them for market. Here, then, is an industry that would actually resuscitate the farming of the kingdom, and keep fourteen millions sterling in our own country which we now pay to the Continent of Europe, independently of our own West Indian colonies, and the industry would employ some thousands of men, women, and children in and around a factory in the months of November, December, and January, when employment in the country districts is almost at a standstill, and would be a benefit to the country in every possible way. If this industry should prove of such advantage to England, how great will it be to Ireland? I feel it would be of the greatest value to that country, and my sincerest hope is that it would create an entirely new industry there, and would in the end falsify Clarendon's remarks on the Irish peasantry which I find in a letter of his to the Earl of Rochester, written on May 4, 1686, more than two hundred years ago:

> It is sad to see the people, I mean the natives, such proper lusty fellows, poor, almost naked, but will work never but when they are ready to starve; and when they have got them a few days' wages will walk about idly till they are gone! If they cannot then get work they steal. Their women do nothing, not so much as spin or knit, but have a cow, two, or three, according to the bigness of their ground, which they milk, and on that they live. Their houses are pig-styes, walls cast up and covered with mud and straw, and out of one of these huts, ten or twelve feet square, you shall see five or six men and women bolt out as you pass by, who stand still, staring about.

Much as I really love the Irish nation, I cannot be blind to their want of thrift and downright laziness.

Mr. Greville in his Memoirs, in 1846, says of the peasantry in the time of the famine :

While they crowd to the overseers with their demands for employment the landowners cannot procure hands, and sturdy beggars, calling themselves destitute, are apprehended with large sums in their pockets. We are here all of one opinion : that some tremendous catastrophe is inevitable, and that there will be some violent convulsion before long.

And in 1872, Thackeray on Killarney, in his 'Irish Sketch Book,' says :

All around the town miserable cabins are stretched. You see people lolling at their doors ; women staring and combing their hair ; men with their little pipes ; children, whose rags hang on only by a miracle, idling in the gutter. Are we to set down all this to absenteeism, and pity poor injured Ireland ? Is the landlord's absence the reason why the house is filthy, and Biddy lolls in the porch all day ? Upon my word, I have heard people talk as if, when Pat's thatch was blown off, the landlord ought to go and fetch the ladder and the straw and mend it himself. People need not be dirty. if they are ever so idle ; if they are ever so poor, pigs and men need not live together. Half an hour's work, and digging a trench, might remove that filthy dunghill from that filthy window. The smoke might as well come out of the chimney as at the door. Why should not Tim do that, as well as walk a hundred and fifty miles to a race ? The priests might do much more to effect these reforms than even the landlords themselves ; and I hope, now that the excellent Father Mathew who has succeeded in arraying his clergy to work with him in the abolition of drunkenness, they will attack the monster dirt with the same goodwill, and surely with the same success.

When I visited Killarney, on my journey to the slob lands of Ennis, there was still much truth in Thackeray's description ; but much improvement has been made, and, if our new industry be a success, very much more will be seen.

Amongst the most pleasing of my reminiscences is that of my acquaintance with the genial Dean Hole, of Rochester. Unless my memory fails me, I first met him when the Royal Agricultural Society held their great annual meeting at Old Trafford, near Manchester. I was one of the implement judges for the society on that occasion, and was there for more than a week before the show opened. It was thought to be a good stroke of policy for the Royal Horticultural Society to hold a meeting for the display of flowers, fruit, &c., at the same time, but the latter was to be quite distinct from the former, and the tents were erected near the entrance of the Agricultural show. There was a fine collection of roses, as it was about the middle of July, and there of course was to be found that famed rosarian. From my early boyhood roses have been my favourite flower, and that bond of sympathy must have drawn us together, and we met afterwards at a dinner given by the mayor to the judges and officials of the Agricultural Society. I have no doubt that, unknown to each other, we had often met in the hunting-field with the Bicester and old Berkshire hounds, when he was an undergraduate at Oxford, and was generally to be found in the first flight, as I can testify. But where the dean excites my warmest admiration is when he is amongst the roses. I had the temerity to send a dozen blooms of that lovely flower to compete in the amateur class, when the Floral Hall attached to the Royal Italian Opera House, Covent Garden, was first opened, and, good as I knew they were, they only received 'a commendation,' and everyone who was, or thought he was, a grower was there. How different were the roses of that day to the present! There were then but few hybrid perpetuals, but the Gallicas and Bourbons were remarkably fine; these are now entirely neglected, but are worthy of a better fate. In a letter I lately had from the dean, he laments with me the neglect of those fine Gallicas, which were at that time unrivalled. The delightful 'Book of the Rose' written by the dean breathes a fervour that is typical of himself, and I know of no book of its kind equal to it. The true classical style, combined as it is with the most careful and practical instruction of 'how to grow' and 'how to show' this beautiful flower, makes it something more than a mere gardening book. The many good stories it contains make the book very readable. I am rather surprised that the learned dean should have passed over the evident love the old Greeks had for this queen of flowers. I remember Sappho speaks of the rose thus:

αἰ τοῖς ἄνθεσιν ἤθελεν ὁ Ζεὺς ἐπιθεῖναι βασιλέα, τὸ ῥόδον ἂν τῶν ἀνθέων ἐβασίλευε. γᾶς ἐστὶ κόσμος, φυτῶν ἀγλάϊσμα, ὀφθαλμὸς ἀνθέων, ἐρύθαμα λειμῶνος, κάλλος ἀστράπτον· ἔρωτος πνέει, Ἀφροδίταν προξενεῖ, εὐειδέσι φύλλοις κομᾷ, εὐκινήτοις πετάλοις τρυφᾷ· τὸ πετάλον τῷ Ζεφύρῳ γελᾷ.

This was translated some years ago by Christopher North in 'Blackwood's Magazine,' line for line, as under:

If Jupiter should wish to impose a sovereign among the flowers, the rose would reign over the flowers. It is the embellishment of the earth, the splendour of plants, the eye of flowers, the meadow's blush—a lightning-flashing beauty. It breathes of love, it hospitably entertains Aphrodite, it waves as locks its leaves beautiful to look on, it luxuriates with easily moved leaves. Its cup laughs to the Zephyr.

COUPE D'HÉBÉ

If the poetess of Mitylene who wrote this about 590 B.C.—*i.e.* nearly 2,500 years ago—could have seen that lovely old rose 'Coupe d'Hébé,' as shown fifty years since, she might have well enough thought that, 'Its cup laughs to the Zephyr,' when Hebe handed the nectar to Jupiter. I hope I shall not be deemed pedantic in recalling this memory of my schooldays; but it so exactly describes my feelings, and doubtless those of the Dean, that I may be perhaps pardoned for interpolating it with my other recollections of early life. It shows, too, how the Greeks almost worshipped the flower, and could they have seen Maréchal Niels, Charles Lefèbres, the Merveille de Lyon, and other roses of the present day, they would indeed have worshipped Τὸ 'Ρόδον as a living deity.

As I have alluded in this chapter to the meeting of the Royal Agricultural Society of England some years ago at Manchester, it may not be out of place to allude to the Jubilee Meeting of the Society, four years since, at Windsor, under the presidency of His Royal Highness the Prince of Wales. The show was held in the Home Park, and was an extraordinary success. I had often thought it a great hardship that old subscribers, who had paid probably over forty years' annual subscriptions of one pound, should still continue payment, while those who, perhaps even as far back as 1840, paid ten guineas became Life Members, and ever after received all the privileges of the Society. I therefore suggested at the previous half-yearly meeting of the Jubilee year, that it would be a graceful act of the Council to elect all those who had paid fifty years' annual subscriptions as 'Life Members.' My friend Sir Jacob Wilson, who is so well known as one of the ablest and most popular members of the Council, warmly supported my proposal, which received the approval of the Prince, and was accepted, and is now a fundamental rule of the Society. As I had paid my fifty years' subscriptions, I was duly elected a Life Member, and I find I am one of only sixteen of that class out of nearly ten thousand ordinary Life Members. I can recall my recollection of the first meeting of the Society at Oxford in 1839, which I attended, and notice the immense advantages afforded to all such institutions by the introduction of railways. I can perfectly remember my father being applied to, one evening in June of that year, to arrange for the reception of some short-horn cattle which were going to the Oxford show. These animals had come in a freight boat from London, by the Aylesbury branch of the Grand Junction Canal. He sent them to the Prebendal Farm, which I some time afterwards tenanted for over thirty years. This farm was alongside the turnpike road to Oxford; and I have not forgotten the beauty of those three animals, which far exceeded in style and character any that I had ever seen before. I have heard that great authority, the late Mr. Strafford, the editor and proprietor of the Herd Book, say 'that no three shorthorns that were ever produced surpassed these, viz., the bull "Duke of Northumberland," the cow "Duchess the 42nd" by "Belvidere," and the heifer, "Duchess the 43rd."' The three animals, I am informed, were driven from Mr. Bates's residence at Kirklevington, in Yorkshire, to Hull, and there shipped to London, then put into the canal boat, and forwarded to Aylesbury. They remained the night, and the next day were driven ten miles to Thame, and finally, the day after, another thirteen miles to Oxford, having been nearly three weeks on the road! What a contrast to the present day! If the renowned 'Tommy Bates,' their owner, now wished to send his cattle to Windsor or Oxford from Darlington, he could put them into a close van, and in twenty-four hours they would reach their destination.

Amongst some old printed papers of mine I discovered an official programme of the first meeting at Oxford, with the names of the President, the Council, the Stewards, and other officials of the Society, with the rules and regulations of the show yard. This printed document was the only known copy extant. I presented it to the Society, who had it framed, and placed it in the committee room at the Jubilee Meeting at Windsor, and it now hangs in the rooms at Hanover Square, as a record of the first meeting of this distinguished Society. It is somewhat singular that it was sent through the post with *a frank*, which is attached, signed by 'T. Acland,' who was then a Member of Parliament, and who, I am glad to say, still lives, and is one of the Trustees, and an active member of the Council. Whilst I am writing this concluding chapter of my recollections, one of the original founders of the Royal Agricultural Society of England, the Right Hon. Sir Harry Verney, Bart., has gone to his long home, in his ninety-fourth year. He was one of my kindest and most revered friends, and was associated with me and the late Duke of Buckingham as a director of the Aylesbury and Buckingham Railway. I am now the only one of the original directors alive of the first board of that small and once despised line, which has now developed into a connecting link of the Metropolitan Railway, and is intended to form a portion of the Manchester, Sheffield, and Lincolnshire line, of which the terminus in London will shortly be completed.

In looking back over these eventful sixty years, I have seen the vicissitudes of many important great families, as well as of my own chequered career; I have seen the disruption and fall of several ministries; and, above all, the romantic and remarkable rise of Lord Beaconsfield. I have watched the commencement and termination of great wars—the Crimean, the Austro-German, the little Germano-Danish, the Turkish and Russian, the Austro-Italian and French, the Chinese, the fratricidal struggle of the North and South in the United States, the great Franco-German, the Egyptian, and numberless other small wars. I remember the flight of Charles X. from France, the monarchy of Louis Philippe, his flight, the formation of the Republic, the Presidency of Louis Napoleon, his elevation as Emperor, his fall, and the establishment of the present Republic. I have not forgotten the misfortunes of our army in Afghanistan, and its destruction in the Kyber Pass, the horrors of the Indian Mutiny, and our disasters in South Africa; and recollect with pride the acquisition of Cyprus, the occupation of Egypt, and the remarkable development of our Colonies under our beloved Queen, for whom, in view of the stirring events of her glorious reign, no better epitaph could be found than that written in St. Paul's Cathedral over the grave of its great architect, Sir Christopher Wren :

'Si monumentum requiris, circumspice.'

www.ingramcontent.com/pod-product-compliance
Lightning Source LLC
Chambersburg PA
CBHW021409230426
43666CB00006B/685